UNIVERSITY OF PENNS

AN EPIGRAPHIC COMMENTARY ON SUETONIUS'S LIFE OF TIBERIUS

BY

CLARA A. HOLTZHAUSSER

A THESIS

PRESENTED TO THE FACULTY OF THE GRADUATE SCHOOL IN
PARTIAL FULFILLMENT OF THE REQUIREMENTS FOR
THE DEGREE OF DOCTOR OF PHILOSOPHY

PHILADELPHIA, PA.
1918

My sincere thanks are expressed to Prof. John C. Rolfe, Prof. Walton B. McDaniel, Prof. Roland G. Kent, Prof. George D. Hadzsits, Prof. Harry B. Van Deventer, Dr. Theodore A. Buenger and Dr. Edward H. Heffner for kindly criticism and advice given in the preparation of this thesis.

INTRODUCTION

The purpose of this thesis is to collect such inscriptions as may either confirm or refute the statements of Suetonius in his *Life of Tiberius*, and such as may prove of general interest in relation to that work. So far as actual historical records are concerned, I find that Suetonius rarely makes a mistake, but the general unfavorable impression that he gives of the attitude of the Roman world towards Tiberius is not confirmed by inscriptions. Although some of the epigraphic records that survive proved an unexpected joy, e. g. that of the sheath and sword of Tiberius found at Mainz, on the other hand there was disappointment in finding no memorials, e. g. of Tiberius from Rhodes or Capri, and none of Piso from Syria.

Such well-known monographs on Tiberius as those of Beesly, Beulé, Pasch, Stahr, Tarver, Thamm, and Wiedemeister afforded practically no help in gathering material for this work. Books that were used only for a special reference are mentioned in full in the body of the paper, while the general bibliography follows.

BIBLIOGRAPHY

Acta soc. arch. Athen. = Πρακτικὰ τῆς ἐν ᾿Αθήναις ᾿Αρχαιολογικῆς ῾Εταιρείας, Athens, 1882–.

Ath. Mitt. = Mitteilungen des kaiserlich. deutschen archäologischen Instituts: Athenische Abteilung, Athens, 1876–1908.

BABELON, E., *Monnaies de la République Romaine*, 2nd ed., Paris, 1885–86.

Bulletin de Correspondance Hellénique, Athens and Paris, 1877–.

COHEN, H., *Description Historique des Monnaies*, vol. I, Paris, 1880.

CIA = Corpus Inscriptionum Atticarum, Berlin, 1873–.

CIG = Corpus Inscriptionum Graecarum, Berlin, 1828–.

CIL = Corpus Inscriptionum Latinarum, Berlin, 1863–.

CURTIUS UND ADLER, *Die Inschriften von Olympia*, Berlin, 1896.

DENNISON, WALTER, *The Epigraphic Sources of the Writings of Gaius Suetonius Tranquillus* (reprint from the American Journal of Archeology, 2nd ser., vol. II, 1898), New York, 1898.

DESSAU, HERMANN, *Inscriptiones Latinae Selectae*, Berlin, 1892–.

ECKHEL, JOSEPH H., *Doctrina Numorum Veterum*, Leipzig.

EGBERT, JAMES C., *Latin Inscriptions* (revised ed. with supplement), New York, 1908.

Ephemeris Epigraphica, Berlin, 1872–.

FISKE, GEORGE CONVERSE, *The Politics of the Patrician Claudii*, Harvard Studies XIII (1902).

FURNEAUX, HENRY, *The Annals of Tacitus*, 2nd ed., Oxford, 1896.

GRAESSE, J. G. Th., *Orbis Latinus*, 2nd ed., Berlin, 1909.

IGR = Inscriptiones Graecae ad Res Romanas Pertinentes, Paris, 1906–1914.

Journal of Hellenic Studies, London 1880–.

KIEPERT, HEINRICH, *Atlas Antiquus*, Berlin.

LIEBENAM, WILLY, *Fasti Consulares*, Bonn, 1909.

Notizie degli Scavi di Antichità Comunicate alla Reale Academia dei Lincei, Rome and Milan, 1876–.

7

PAULY-WISSOWA, *Real-Encyclopädie*, Stuttgart, 1894–.

PLATNER, SAMUEL B., *Topography and Monuments of Ancient Rome*, 2nd ed., Boston, 1911.

Prosopographia Imperii Romani, Berlin, 1897–98.

Revue Archéologique, Paris, 1844–.

RUSHFORTH, G. M., *Latin Historical Inscriptions*, Oxford, 1893.

SMITH, *Dictionary of Greek and Roman Biography and Mythology*, London, 1844–49.

An Epigraphic Commentary on Suetonius's Life of Tiberius

I.1.[1]

gens...orta est ex Regillis: In support of this statement we find in the Fasti Cos. Capitolini for the years B. C. 451, 450 the name Ap. Claudius Ap. f., M. n. Crass. Inrigill. Sabin. II; and for the year B. C. 362 *Ap. Claudius P. f., Ap. n. Crassus* Inregillensis dict.: CIL I², pp. 16, 20. Forcellini in his *Onomasticon* justifies the reading *Inregillensis.*

I.2.

triumphos sex, duas ouationes: These numbers, evidently not including Tiberius's triumphs (cf. IX. 2, XVII. 1, XX.), are almost completely confirmed by the Acta Triumph. Capitolina, which cite six triumphs and one ovation: B. C. 273 *C. Claudius* ...f., C. n. Canina; B. C. 268 Ap. Claudius Ap. f., C. *n. Rufus;* B. C. 222 M. Claudius M. f., M. n. Marcellus; B. C. 196 *M.* Claud*ius M. f., M. n.* Marcellus; B. C. 174 *Ap. C*laudius C. *f., Ap. n. Centho* ovans; B. C. 166 *M. C*laudius M. f., M. n. Marcellus; B. C. 155 *M. Claudius M. f.,* M. n. Marcellus: CIL I², pp. 46–48.

II.1.

Appius Caecus...dissuasit: His elogium reads: Appius Claudius | C. f. Caecus | censor, cos. bis, dict., interrex III, | pr. II, aed. cur. II, q., tr. mil. III. Com|plura oppida de Samnitibus cepit; | Sabinorum et Tuscorum exerci|tum fudit; pacem fieri cum Tyrrho (*sic*) | rege prohibuit. In censura viam | Appiam stravit et aquam in | urbem adduxit; aedem Bellona*e* | fecit: CIL I², p. 192. His name appears also in the Fasti Cos. Capitolini: B. C. 312 Cens. Ap. Claudius C. f., Ap. n. Caecus; B. C. 307 Ap. Claudius C. f., Ap. n. Caecus: CIL I², p. 21.

Claudius Caudex: The Fasti Cos. Capitolini record his name for the year B. C. 264: Ap. Claudius C. f., Ap. n. Caudex: CIL I², p. 22.

---

[1] The notes follow the order of the text, the numbers denoting the chapter and section in Ihm's edition.

† **Tibus Nero...Hasdrubalem...oppressit:** According to Liv. XXVII. 51. 8, 11 it was C. Claudius (Nero) who defeated Hasdrubal. Polyb. XI. 1 calls him only Claudius, and Appian *Hannib.* 52, only Nero. The Fasti Cos. Capitolini mention both men: for the year B. C. 207, C. Claudius Ti. f., Ti. n. Nero; B. C. 204, Cens. C. Claudius Ti. f., Ti. n. Nero l(ustrum) f(ecit) XXXXV; for B. C. 202, Ti. Claudius P. f., Ti. n. Nero: CIL I², p. 23. Tiberius as consul is mentioned also in CIL XIV. 2239 from the Alban Mount (which, in the restored portion, seems to err in making Servilius, colleague of Tiberius, the grandson of Gaius).

II.2.

Claudius Regillianus decemuir legibus scribendis: The Fasti Cos. Capitolini for the year B. C. 451 confirm his decem-virate: Ap. Claudius Ap. f., M. n. Crass. Inrigill. Sabin. II, T. Genuc*ius L. f., L. n.* Aug*u*rinus | abdicarunt ut d*e*cemviri con-sular*i imperio fier*ent. | decemviri consular*i imp*erio legibus scr*ibundis fac*ti eod. anno | Ap. Claudius Ap. f., M. n. Crassus Inr*igill. Sab*in. qui cos. fuer*at* etc.; and for B. C. 450 name him again, CIL I², p. 16.

Claudius Pulcher...(dictatorem) Glycian uiatorem suum dixit: This statement, too, is supported by the Fasti Cos. Capitolini for the year B. C. 249: P. Claudius Ap. f., C. n. Pulcher, L. Iunius C. f., L. n. Pullus. | M. Claudius C. f. Glicia, qui scriba fuerat, dictator coact(i) abdic(are) | sine mag. eq. in eius locum factus est: CIL I², p. 24.

II.3.

Claudia...quae nauem....extraxit: Several inscriptions in honor of the Mother of the Gods and the ship Salvia may have been dedicated by persons having this incident in mind: Matri deum | et navi Salviae | Q. Nunnius | Telephus mag. | col. culto. eius | d. s. d. d.: CIL VI. 494; cf. 492, 493. In connection with the coming of the Magna Mater to Rome, the Fasti Prae-nestini for April 4 offer an interesting notice: Ludi M(atri) D(eum) M(agnae) I(daeae) Megalensia vocantur quod ea dea | Megale appellatur. Nobilium mutitationes cenarum | solitae sunt frequenter fieri quod Mater Magna | ex libris Sibullinis arcessita locum mutavit ex Phrygia | Romam: CIL I², p. 235; cf. Fasti Maff., p. 224, Philoc., p. 262.

II.4.

uirgo Vestalis fratrem....prosecuta est: The brother, or father as Cicero *Cael.* 34 and Valerius Maximus 5. 4. 6. say, was probably Ap. Clau*dius C. f., Ap. n. Pul*cher mentioned in the Fasti Cos. Capitolini for the year B. C. 143: CIL I², p. 26.

III.1.

paternum (genus) a Tiberio Nerone: At least one inscription, found at Centumcellae, gives evidence that both Tiberius's father and his grandfather were named Tiberius Nero: *Ti. Claudio Ti.* f., *Ti. n.* Neroni | *pontifici* | ...optimi | *princ*ipis | ... ? *imperi R*omani: CIL XI. 3517.

insertus est et Liuiorum familiae etc.: The names of both Tiberius's maternal grandparents are preserved in inscriptions from Marruvium, that of his grandfather evidently verifying the adoption into the family of the Livii: M. Livius D*ru*s*us* Claudia*nus:* CIL IX. 3660; Alfidia M. f. mater Augustae: CIL IX. 3661; cf. II. 1667.

They are recorded also in two Greek inscriptions from Samos, found on the bases of statues set up in honor of Livia's parents: ὁ δῆμος | Μάρκον Λίβιον Δροῦσον τὸν | πατέρα θεᾶς 'Ιουλίας Σεβασ|τῆς μεγίστων ἀγαθῶν αἴτιον|γεγονότα τῷ κόσμῳ: IGR 4.982; ὁ δῆμος|'Αλφιδίαν τὴν μη|τέρα θεᾶς 'Ιουλίας|Σεβαστ[ῆ]ς, μεγίσ|των ἀγαθῶν αἰτίαν| γεγονυῖαν τῷ κόσ|μῳ: IGR 4.983.

III.2.

Salinator: Both his consulship and his censorship are confirmed by the Fasti Cos. Capitolini, for the year B. C. 207: M. Livius M. f., M. n. Salinator *II;* M. Livius M. f., M. n. Salinator dict.; and for B. C. 204: Cens. M. Livius M. f., M. n. Salinator: CIL I², p. 23.

Drusus: The Fasti Cos. Capitolini for the year B. C. 147 name C. Livius M. Aimiliani f., M. *n.* Drusus: CIL I², p. 26. It is possible that the grandfather here indicated may represent the original Drusus, although that would make him a generation too late to account for the *abnepos* mentioned a few lines below.

eius abnepos...filium reliquit, quem...diuersa factio ...interemit: The elogium of this son bears witness to his political activity and to his death in office: M. Livius M. f., C.

n. Drusus pontifex, | tr. mil., X vir stlit. iudic., | tr. pl., X vir
a. d. a lege sua | et eodem anno V vir a. d. a lege Saufeia | in
magistratu occisus est: CIL I², p. 199.

IV.1.

Pater Tiberi, Nero: We have an inscription naming Ti-
berius's father as such: Ti. Claudius Nero pater | Ti. Caesaris
Aug.: CIL IX. 3662 from Marruvium; and another, given
among false inscriptions, which we could wish were genuine,
especially since Nero is here called pontifex: Ti. Claudio Ti. f.
Ner ... | ...pr., pontifici m... | patri Ti. Caesaris | conleg ...
pont....Combult.. | ....d. d.: CIL X. 530*.

IV.3.

Liuiam Drusillam: There are at least two inscriptions
recording the name Livia Drusilla, one Latin, found in the pave-
ment of the Via Ostiensis: L. Aurelius Cottae l., | Philostra |
Leivia | Drusillae | l. Galatea | in fr. p. XII, in | ag. XX; h. | ..:
CIL VI. 13179; the other Greek, from Thasos, in which Julia,
the daughter of Augustus, and Julia, the daughter of Marcus
Agrippa, also are honored: ὁ δῆμος | Ἰουλίαν Καίσαρος Σεβαστοῦ | θυγα-
τέρα τὴν ἀ[πὸ] προγόνων | εὐεργέτιν. | ὁ δῆμος | Λειβίαν Δρού[σιλλαν τὴ]ν τοῦ
Σεβαστοῦ Καίσαρος | γυναῖκα θεὰν εὐεργέτιν. | Ἰουλίαν Μάρκου Ἀγ[ρ]ίππου
θυγατέρα | ὁ δῆμος: IGR 1.835.

V.

**XVI. Kal. Dec. M. Aemilio Lepido iterum L. Munatio
Planco conss.:** This date is confirmed by at least two calen-
dars—the Antian: XVI. K. Dec. Ti. Aug. natal.: CIL I², p.
249 = X. 6638; the Cumaean: XVI. K. Decembr. Natalis Ti.
Caesaris: CIL X. 8375. Lepidus and Plancus are both named
in the Acta Triumph. Capitolina for the year B. C. 43, CIL I²,
p. 50, and in the Fasti Colotiani for B. C. 42, CIL I², p. 64.
Several inscriptions besides these, and coins, record Plancus's
name: two inscriptions from Rome, one of a slave, the other of
a freedwoman, CIL VI. 22668, 22670; one from Formiae commemorating his building a shrine of Saturn, his dividing fields
in Italy, his spoils of war, and his founding the colonies Lugdunum and Raurica, CIL X. 6087; a fragmentary one on a
piece of marble dug up near the arch of Septimius Severus, CIL
VI. 1316; one mentioning a statue of him, CIL VI. 9673 (cf.

VI. 10023); a Greek inscription, honoring him for his goodness and kindness, Acta soc. arch. Athen. 1885, p. 26; coins recording his being called imperator, Babelon I, p. 178. 57, pro-consul, ib. 58, 59, and praefectus urbanus, Babelon II, p. 239. 1, 2, 3.

VI.4.

Troiam circensibus lusit: It is interesting to note in connection with this an inscription from Olympia which records Tiberius's victory in a four-horse chariot race, between the years B. C. 20 and B. C. 8: Τιβέριον Κλαύδιον Τι[βε]|ρίου υἱὸν Νέρωνα, νική|σαντα 'Ολύμπια τεθρίππῳ τελείῳ...|...| 'Απολλ[ώ]νιος 'Απολλωίου ὑὸς|'Ηλεῖος ὁ καὶ Τιβέριος [Κλ]αύδιος| τὸν ἑαυτοῦ πάτρωνα καὶ εὐεργέτην, Διὶ 'Ολυμπίῳ: Curtius u. Adler 220.

VII.1.

Virili toga sumpta: The very day of this happy occasion, Apr. 24, B. C. 27, is known to us from the Fasti Praenestini: VIII. K. Mai Ti. Caesar togam virilem sumpsit imp. Caesare VII M. Agrippa | III cos.: CIL I², p. 236.

VII.2.

Agrippinam: We have at least two inscriptions dedicated to her, one from Laus Pompeia: Agrippinae | M. Agrippae f., | Drusi Caesar. matri | !!!!!! | !!!!!! | d. d., (in which the words erased probably were *C. Asini Galli | uxori*, Asinius being the second husband of Agrippina): CIL V. 6359; another from Telesia: *Vipsaniae M. Agrippae f. Agrippi*nae, Drusi | *Caes. matri*, *aviae Ti. et Germanici Caes.*, divi Aug. pron(epotum): CIL IX. 2201. CIL VI. 9901 a is in honor of a freedman of Agrippina.

sublato....filio Druso: A calendar from Cumae records the date of his birth: Nonis Octobr. Drusi Caesaris natalis: CIL X. 8375. Several other inscriptions, dedicated to him, give either simply his name or little more, CIL III. 5764 from Raetia, 13565 from Crete; V. 2151 = VI. 908; XIV. 84; also three Greek inscriptions, IGR 3.895 from Cilicia, dedicated by a freedman; IGR 4.324 from Pergamum, 930 from Chios, dedicated by the people.

VII.3.

Drusum fratrem in Germania amisit: In the Fasti Oppiani Maiores we have: XIIX. K. Oct. Inferiae Drusi Caesaris: CIL VI. 32493; and likewise in the Fasti Antiates for the same day: Infer. Dr*usi:* CIL I², p. 248; but Mommsen's conclusion that this was the day on which Drusus died, though probable, seems hardly justified in its finality, since *inferiae* were offered on other days than the anniversary of the death (cf. Comm. Diurni under this day, CIL I², p. 329). A few inscriptions of Drusus are quite simple, dedicated to him alone: CIL V. 3109 from Vicetia, 4310 from Brixia; CIA 3.443, on a marble base in an arch north of the Erectheum, dedicated by the people. Several name him as the brother of Tiberius: CIL IX. 3663 from Marruvium; Dessau 8787 from near Troy; CIL IX. 2443 from Saepinum, only in naming both Drusus and Tiberius as the sons of Tiberius; and, in so far as they are dedicated to Livia as the mother of both Tiberius and Drusus, CIL II. 2038 from Anticaria; IX. 3304 from Superaequum; XI. 1165 from Veleia. As for his activities in Germany, Suetonius tells us (*Claud.* I. 3) that he received the cognomen Germanicus after his death, and a number of inscriptions confirm this statement: CIL II. 2038; IX. 2443, 3304, 3663; Eph. Ep. 4.775; IGR 1.1025; also several coins listed by Cohen, bearing the following inscription: Nero Claudius Drusus Germanicus imp. de Germanis: 1, pp. 220, 221. 1–6. There are also two inscriptions of Claudius commemorating his building of the Via Claudia Augusta, which record that Drusus, his father, had laid out this road after the Alps had been opened as a result of war: CIL V. 8002, 8003.

VIII.

regem Archelaum...defendit: A Greek inscription dedicated to Archelaus by the people has been found in Athens west of the Parthenon: [ὁ] δῆμος | [βασιλέα Καπ]παδοκί[ας καὶ τῆς| τραχεία]ς Κιλικίας Ἀ[ρχέλαον | φι]λόπατριν ἀρε[τῆς]| ἕνεκα: CIA 3.545. Ib. 546 was dedicated by the Council; and one of his coins is to be found in Eckhel 3, p. 201.

Varrone Murena: (Cf. *Aug.* XIX. 1, LVI. 4, LXVI. 3). Varro's name appears in the Fasti Cos. Capitolini for the year B. C. 23, CIL I,² p. 28; on a marble tablet dedicated to him and found at Lanuvium, CIL XIV. 2109; on a column found between the seventh milestone of the Via Latina and the seventh of the Via Labicana, for which Varro and Trebellius as curule aediles granted the site, CIL VI. 1324.

IX.1.

expeditione Cantabrica: Several inscriptions from Spain, dedicated by colonists or by private individuals to Tiberius, not yet Caesar, as patron, may have been a result of this expedition: Ti. Claudio Ti. *f.* | Neroni, | patrono, colon*i:* CIL II. 5930; cf. ib. 1113, 1529, 6080.

regnum Armeniae Tigrani restituit: Augustus records this event in the Monumentum Ancyranum, giving due credit to Tiberius, who was then his stepson: Armeniam maiorem inter|fecto rege eius Artax*e cu*m possem facere provinciam, malui maiorum | nostrorum exemplo reg*nu*m id Tigrani regis Artavasdis filio, nepoti au|tem Tigranis regis, per T*i. Ne*ronem tra*dere*, qu*i tum* mihi privignus erat: 5.24–27, CIL III, p. 782. There are, too, a number of coins struck in commemoration of the victory, bearing the name, not of Tiberius, who was merely the agent in the affair, but of Augustus, under whose auspices it was undertaken: Augustus, Armenia capta: Cohen 1, p. 64. 8–12; cf. also ib. p. 71. 56–59; p. 113. 360, 361; p. 134. 487–489.

recepit et signa, quae M. Crasso ademerant Parthi: This, too, Augustus records, though without mention of Tiberius: Parthos trium exercitum Romano|rum spolia et signa re*ddere* mihi supplicesque amicitiam populi Romani | petere coegi: Mon. Ancyr. 5. 40–42, CIL III, p. 782. And this victory, too, is commemorated by coins, some bearing the simple inscription Caesar Augustus, signis Parthicis receptis, Cohen 1, p. 99. 255–263; p. 100. 264–268; cf., also, p. 112, 358; p. 113. 359; p. 133. 484, 485; p. 134. 486; others have a more elaborate statement: S. P. Q. R. Imp. Caesari Aug. cos. XI, tr. pot. VI, civib. et sign. milit. a Part. recuper.: ib. p. 75. 82–85; cf. p. 103, 298.

Raeticum Vindelicumque bellum...gessit: At Mainz there was found a sheath, splendidly ornamented, together with a sword which lacked its hilt. They are now in the British Museum. On the sheath appear Germanicus, returning as a victor; Mars; Tiberius sitting on a throne, in his outstretched right hand holding a figure of Victory and leaning his left arm on a shield on which is written Felicitas Tiberi; and Victory, on whose shield is written Vic. Aug. In the middle of the sheath is a figure of Tiberius, crowned with laurel, represented, within a laurel wreath, upon a shield-formed surface; below, a small building with an eagle and standards; and still farther below, an Amazon, holding in her left hand a spear, in her right, a battle-axe. Because of the Amazon here represented, in view of Horace *Carm.* 4. 4. 20, this relic has been connected with the campaign of Tiberius and Drusus against the Vindelici in B. C. 15, but the interpretation is not final: CIL XIII. 6796.

(bellum)...Pannonicum...(gessit): For this victory Tiberius, stepson and lieutenant general of Augustus, receives due credit: Pannoniorum gentes, qua*s a*nte me principem populi Romani exercitus nun|quam ad*i*t, devictas per Ti. *N*eronem, qui tum erat pri*v*ignu*s e*t legatus meus, | imperio populi Romani sub*i*eci: Mon. Ancyr. 5. 44–46, CIL III, p. 782.   It may be of interest to note that a broken bit of vessel or, it may be, of pipe has been found in Pannonia, bearing the letters Ti. Ca...: CIL III. 10849.

Germanicum (bellum) gessit: Velleius 2. 104. 3, 4 speaks of the joy with which Tiberius's coming into Germany was greeted, and it seems quite probable that the following inscription from Bagacum, which must be dated between 4 and 14 A. D., the years in which, respectively, Tiberius was adopted by Augustus, and Augustus died, was dedicated as an expression of this feeling, and with reference, perhaps, to this particular campaign: Ti. Caesari Augusti f. | divi nepoti adventui | eius sacrum | Cn. Licinius C. f. Vol. Navos: CIL XIII. 3570.

IX.2.

Dalmatas subegit: That Dalmatia remained conquered and under Roman control and care during Tiberius's reign is shown by a number of inscriptions, several of which testify to Tiberius's activity in building roads there: V. | *Ti. Caesar divi Augusti* f. | *Au*gustus imp., pont. max., | *trib*. potest. XIIX, cos. II, | *viam* a Colonia Salonitan | ...*m*unit...*m*unit ad *sum*mum montem Ditionum | Ulcirum per millia passuum | a Salonis LXXVIID | P. Dolabella leg. pro | pr.: CIL III. 3198 (cf. 10156), also 3199 (cf. 10157), 3200, 3201 (cf. 10159). One of these is dedicated by the seventh and eleventh legions: Ti. Caesar divi Aug. f. | Augustus imp., pontif. max., | trib. potest.

XX, cos. III. | leg. VII, leg. XI, | P. Cornelio Dolabella | leg. pro pr.: CIL III. 2908; while three are dedicated to Lucius Volusius Saturninus, an officer of Tiberius in Dalmatia: L. Volusio L. f. Saturnino | cos., aug., sodali Augustali, | sodali Titio, *leg., pro pr. divi Aug.* | leg. pro pr. Ti. *Caesaris Augusti:* CIL III. 2974, also 2975, 14322. At least one tile found in Dalmatia bears Tiberius's name: Ti. Pansiana: CIL III. 3213.3.

IX.3.

maturius incohauit...consulatum: The name of Tiberius in his first consulship (B. C. 13), together with that of his colleague, Quintilius Varus, appears in various inscriptions: in the Fasti Amiternini for July 4, fer(iae) ex s(enatus) c(onsulto) q(uod) e(o) d(ie) ara Pacis Aug. in camp. Mar. constituta est, Nerone et Varo cos.: CIL I², p. 244; in the Fasti Colotiani, CIL I², p. 64, the Biondiani, ib. p. 65; on two amphorae, one, found on the Esquiline, recording the pouring of wine that had been pressed in the consulship of the two Lentuli (B. C. 18): Ti. Claudio P. Quinctilio cos. | a. d. XIII. K. Iun. vinum | diffusum quod natum est | duobus Lentulis cos., | autocr(atum): CIL XV. 4539, the other found in the ditch of the agger near the castra Praetoria, CIL XV. 4575; also on one of the pieces of pottery bearing the names of the consuls of the year, found near Placentia, CIL I¹. 798 = XI.6673.22; in an inscription recording the celebration, in accordance with a decree of the senate, by Varus, together with his colleague Tiberius, of games to Jupiter Optimus Maximus, because of the return of Augustus from Spain and Gaul, CIL VI. 386; and, further, in CIL VI. 850, 9290, the last three from Rome; IX. 2197 from Telesia.

consul iterum: For this consulship, too, we have the evidence of several inscriptions, in some of which the names of Tiberius and his colleague, Gnaeus Calpurnius Piso, are used simply to fix the date (B.C. 7): CIL I¹. 747 on one of the tesserae consulares; Mon. Ancyr. 3.28, CIL III. p. 778; on an amphora from Cherium, CIL V. 8112.83; CIL VI. 7461 from Rome; IX. 5308 from Cupra maritima; X. 924 from Pompeii. In CIL IX. 2443 Tiberius is given, besides other titles, that of consul for the second time, and the same title occurs in CIL VI. 385, which it might be interesting to quote in full: Ti. Claudius Ti. f. Nero | pontifex, cos. iterum, | imp. iterum | ludos votivos pro reditu | Imp. Caesaris divi f. Augusti | pontificis maximi | Iovi Optimo Maximo fecit | ex s. c. (cf. CIL VI. 386 supra). It is evident in this inscription that after the seventh line, one line has been carefully erased, which read about as follows: cum Cn. Calpurnio Pisone conlega: cf. CIL VI. 30751.

tribuniciam potestatem in quinquennium accepit: The record of this first tenure of tribunician power is preserved in an inscription from Samnium, which must be dated between the years B. C. 2 and A. D. 4: Ti. Claudius Ti. f. Nero pont., cos. II, *imp.* I (?), trib. po*t*est. V, Nero Claudius Ti. f. Drusus Ger*ma*n*icus* augur, *cos.*, *imp.* murum, portas, turris d(e) s(ua) p(ecunia) f(aciendas) c(uraverunt): CIL IX. 2443 (cf. supra).

X.1.

M. Agrippae qui...Mytilenas abierat: A number of Greek inscriptions, most of which honor Agrippa as savior, or as savior and founder, have been found at Mytilene: ὁ δᾶμος | θεὸν σωτῆρα τᾶς πόλιος Μάρκον | 'Αγρίππαν τὸν εὐεργέταν καὶ κτίσταν: IGR 4.21; cf. also IGR 4.65 b, 67 c, 68 b, 69, 70, 78 a, 79 g.

XII.2.

Gaium Orienti praepositum: It seems quite likely that Gaius's governorship of the Orient was responsible for the following inscription from Ilium, in which he is honored by both the Council and the people: ἡ βουλὴ καὶ ὁ δῆμος | Γάϊον Καίσαρα τὸν υἱὸν τοῦ Σεβασ|τοῦ τὸν συγγενῆ καὶ πατρῶνα καὶ εὐ|εργέτην τῆς πόλεως: IGR 4.205.

M. Lolli: His name appears on the bridge leading from the city of Rome to the island: M. Lollius M. f. Q. Lepid*us M'*. f. *cos.* ex s. c. probaverunt: CIL VI. 1305; and also on a marble base west of the Parthenon at Athens: ἡ βουλὴ | Μάρκον Λόλλιο[ν]| ἀρετῆς ἕνεκ[α]: CIA 3.584.

XIV.3.

Geryonis oraculum: More than fifteen lots have been found which may have come from this oracle, but as yet their provenance is a matter of doubt. A few may serve to show the general nature of all, particularly their extreme, though, of course, necessary, indefiniteness: conrigi vix tandem quod | curvom est factum *c*rede: CIL I¹. 1438; credis quod deicunt non | sunt ita ne fore stultu: CIL I¹. 1439; de incerto certa ne fiant | si sapis caveas: CIL I¹. 1440; also 1441–1454.

in Aponi fontem talos aureos iaceret: Though we have not, so far as I know, any of the dice left today, we have a number of inscriptions dedicated to these waters, of which the following is an example: C. Acutius | C. f. Maturus | A(pono) A(ugusto) — or A(quis) A(poni)— v(otum) s(olvit) l(ibens) m(erito): CIL V. 2783; also 2784-2790, 8990.

XIV.4.

Thrasyllum: There is an inscription from Smyrna of a Tiberius Claudius Thrasyllus, who is thought by Hirschfeld to have been the astrologer: *Ti. Claudius Ti. Claudi* Thrasylli *l...* | *Ti. Caesari Augusto et Augustae Caes. Aug. matri* | Τιβέριος Κλαύδι]ος Τιβερίου Κλα[υδίου Θρασύλλου ἀπελεύθερος...Τιβερίῳ | Καίσαρι Σεβαστῷ κ]αὶ Σεβαστῇ Καί[σαρος Σεβαστοῦ μητρί]: CIL III. 7107 = IGR 4.1392.

XV.1.

deducto in forum filio Druso: That Drusus took an active part in public life is evident from the many inscriptions either dedicated to him or containing his name in some connection. We learn that he was one of the Arval Brothers (CIL VI. 2023 a), that he was augur, pontifex maximus, quaestor, flamen of Augustus, one of the Sodales Augustales, one of the quindecimviri sacris faciendis, quinquennalis, consul twice, and holder of the tribuncian power twice: CIL II. 3103, 3829, both from Tarraconensis, 5048 from Baetica; V. 4954 from Camunni, 6416.2 from Ticinum; VI. 910, 31280, both from Rome; IX. 35 from Brundisium; X. 3694 from Cumae, 4573 from Caiatia, 4617 from Cubulteria, 4638 from Cales, 5393.12, 5394.6, both from Aquinum, 6639.11 from Antium; XI. 3787(?) from Veii, 4777 from Spoletium, 6689.119 (in tegulis) from Tifernum Tiberinum; XII. 147 from Nantuates, 1847 from Vienna (Vienne on the Rhone); XIII. 1036 (on a triumphal arch in Aquitania, dedicated to Germanicus and to Tiberius together with Drusus); XIV. 2964. II. 5 from Praeneste; Eph. Ep. 7. 1236. He even celebrated a triumph in 20 A. D., as is known from CIL XIV. 244 from Ostia: M. Valerius Messalla, M. Aur*elius Cotta cos.* | V. K. Iun. Drusus *Caesar* | triumphavit ex Ill*yrico.* Though in most of the inscriptions containing his name, and dedicated after Tiberius's adoption by Augustus, Drusus is called *Drusus Caesar*, yet his full name seems to have been *Drusus Iulius Caesar*, as it appears in at least two inscriptions, one from Rome: Druso Iulio Ti. f., | Augusti nepoti | Caesari: CIL VI. 908 = V. 2151; the other from Halicarnassus, inscribed in his father's honor as well as in his own: Τιβερίου ᾽Ιουλίου | Καίσαρος | καὶ Δρούσου | ᾽Ιουλίου Καίσαρος | ᾽Αρχίδαμος Νικομάχου ἐποίησεν: CIG 2657.

XV.2.

Gaio et Lucio intra triennium defunctis: An inscription from Gabii names September 19, 2 A. D. as the day of the death of Lucius Caesar, and February 21, 4 A. D. as that of Gaius's death: *P. Vinucius* L. Alfenius | . . . *L. Caesar* decessit XIII. K. Oct. | Sex. Aelius C. Sentius | . . . C. Caesar decessit VIIII. K. *Martias:* CIL XIV. 2801.   CIL IX. 5290 from Cupra maritima corroborates the date of Gaius's death; but the Fasti Antiates record: XIII. K. Sept. Infer. L. Caesaris: CIL I², p. 248.   As we have said above (VII. 3), the *inferiae* did not always mark the death-day, but in view of *Aug.* LVX. 1, where we are told that Augustus lost Gaius and Lucius within a space of eighteen months, the earlier date, August 20, would seem to be correct. Gaius's sepulchral inscription from Rome is still preserved: ossa | C. Caesaris Augusti f. | principis iuventutis: CIL VI. 884.

adoptatur ab Augusto: The exact day of Tiberius's adoption, June 26, 4 A. D., is recorded by the Fasti Amiternini: VI. K. Iul. fer(iae) ex s. c., quod eo die *imp.* | Augus*tus adoptavit sibi* | filiu*m Ti. Caesarem* | Aelio *et Sentio cos.:* CIL I², p. 243.   In CIL IX. 5290, l. 7, Mommsen seems wrongly to have restored the date to V. K. Iul., relying, perhaps, on Vell. 2.103, where the error may easily be due to a scribe.   After his adoption Tiberius is known usually as Tiberius Caesar, and, after the death of Augustus, as Tiberius Caesar Augustus (at least on coins and inscriptions); but there are no fewer than three inscriptions in which the gentile name *Iulius* is retained, one from the province of Baetica: Herculi Invicto | Ti. Iulius Augusti f., divi nep. Caesar Aug. | imp., pontifex maximus ded. | !!!!!!!! : CIL II. 1660; another, a formal decree of Vespasian, in which Tiberius's name appears five times: CIL VI. 930, ll. 2, 5, 20, 23, 26; the third, a Greek inscription from Crete: Τιβέριον ᾽Ιούλιον | [Σ]εβαστοῦ υἱόν: IGR 1.958.

simul cum. . .M. Agrippa: One inscription, at least, definitely testifies to his adoption: Agrippa Iulius | Augusti f., div

n. | Caesar: CIL X. 405 from Volcei. There are a few others dedicated to him evidently before 4 A. D.: CIL II. 1528 from Baetica; X. 924 from Pompeii, 1240 from Nola. Another, from Forum Clodi, giving his age as seven years, must be assigned to B. C. 5: M. Agrippae M. f. | Augusti nepoti, | annos nato VII, | A. Octavius A. f. Ligus, | M. Genicilius M. f. Sabin. II vir.: CIL XI. 3305. The name of a steward of Agrippa, Atticus, is preserved in CIL VI. 8820 from Rome.

coactus prius ipse Germanicum...adoptare: In the greater number of the many inscriptions dedicated to Germanicus, or mentioning him, he appears as Germanicus Caesar, Ti. Aug. f.; cf., e. g., CIL II. 1517, 2039, 2198, 3104, all from the province of Baetica; III. 334 from Apamea; V. 4308 from Brixia, 6416.3 from Ticinum; VI. 921 b, 923, 924, all from Rome; X. 460 from Lucania, 513 from Salernum, 1415 from Herculaneum; XI. 3306, 3308 both from Forum Clodi, 3786 from Veii, 4776 from·Spoletium, 5224 from Fulginiae, 6321 from Pisaurum; XIII. 1036 from Aquitania, XIV. 83 from Ostia, 3942 from Nomentum; XV, p. 995.1 on a lead tessera, found in the Tiber; IGR 3.715 from Lycia; 4.11 from Eresus, 326 from Pergamum.

XVI.1.

Parthorum legati mandatis Augusto Romae redditis: The embassy of the Parthians is recorded by Augustus, though no mention is made of their having been required to appear before Tiberius: a me gentes Parthorum et Medoru*m per legatos* principes earum gen|tium reges pet*i*tos acceperunt: Mon. Ancyr. 6. 9, 10, CIL III, p. 784.

XVI.2.

+toto Illyrico...perdomito et in dicionem redacto: Tiberius's victory in Illyricum is noted in the Fasti Antiates: III. Non. Aug. Ti. Aug. Inlyrico vic.: CIL I², p. 248. Augustus, too, records it, but without mention of Tiberius: protuli... fines Il*l*yrici ad r*i*pam fluminis | Dan*u*i: Mon. Ancyr. 5. 46, 47, CIL III, p. 782. Whereas Suetonius's statement makes the date when the Danube became a boundary of Roman conquest at least as late as 6 A. D., the Mon. Ancyr. appears to put it fully fifteen years earlier, and Dio 50.24 even before B. C. 31.

There seems to be no authority for the spelling *Danubium*, which appears in one of the manuscripts of Suetonius. The

epigraphic evidence favors *Danuvium*: cf. e. g. CIL III. 3416,
3676 both from Lower Pannonia, 5755 from Noricum, 5863
from Raetia; VI. 32755 from Rome.

XVII.1.

**Quintilius Varus cum tribus legionibus in Germania
periit:** An inscription from Xanten identifies the 18th legion
as one of Varus's: M. Caelius | M. l. | Privatus. | M. Caelius |
M. l. | Thiaminus. | M. Caelio T. f. Lem(onia tribu), Bon(onia),
Ɔ leg. XIIX, ann. LIII. | *ce*cidit bello Variano. ossa | *inferre*
licebit. P. Caelius Te (*sic*) Lem(onia tribu) frater fecit: CIL
XIII. 8648. This legion, together with the 19th, mentioned
by Tac. *Ann.* 1. 60. 4, and the 17th, which appears not to have
been heard of after the disaster, are probably the three that
perished. From Pergamum we have two Greek inscriptions
dedicated to Varus by the people: ὁ δῆμος | Πόπλιον Κοιντίλιον
Σέ[ξ]του υἱὸν Οὐᾶρον | πάσης ἀρετῆ[ς ἕνεκ]α: IGR 4.418; also 419.

XVII.2.

censuerunt...alii ut Invictus...cognominaretur: In
the Fasti Amiternini under May 26 is a fragmentary record
which Mommsen thinks may pertain to this passage in Suetonius, and if so, may be supplemented about as follows: *fer.
ex s. c. quo*d eo die | *a senatu Ti.* Caesar | *appellatus* invictus est|
nec accepit: CIL IX, p. 698, note to n. 4192.

XVIII.1.

Proximo anno repetita Germania: It was probably in
honor of this campaign that a coin, proclaiming Tiberius imperator for the fifth time, was struck in 10 A. D.: Ti. Caesar
August. f. imperat. V, pontifex, tribun. potestate XII: Cohen
I, p. 192. 27. It is possible that the inscription, quoted under
IX. 1 with reference to the war in Germany, may be assigned to
the time of this campaign.

XX.

triumphum...egit: The Fasti Praenestini note the cele-
bration of this triumph: XVII. K. Feb. Ti. Caesar ex Pan*nonia
et Delmatia triumpha*vit: CIL I², p. 231. Probably the same
ceremony, too, is commemorated on coins, struck in 13, 14, 15
A. D., which depict Tiberius seated in a triumphal chariot

drawn by four horses, holding in one hand a laurel branch, in the other a sceptre with an eagle, and bear the inscription Ti. Caesar Aug. f., tr. pot. XV (others XVI, XVII), Caesar Augustus divi f. pater patriae: Eck. 6, p. 186.

legatis...triumphalia ornamenta impetrarat: A memorial from Tibur of at least one of these generals, proclaiming the winning of the triumphal regalia, has been preserved: M. Plautius M. f., A. n. | Silvanus, | cos., VII vir epulon., | huic senatus triumphalia | ornamenta decrevit | ob res in Ilyrico | bene gestas. | Lartia Cn. f. uxor. | A. Plautius M. f. | Urgulanius | vixit ann. IX: CIL XIV. 3606; cf. 3605.

Batonem Pannonium ducem: Bato's name is preserved in a fragmentary inscription from Verona, which belonged, evidently, to some officer who took part in this war: ...*bello* | Batoniano praefuit | Iapudiai et Liburn., | sibi et libertis | t(estamento) f(ieri) i(ussit): CIL V. 3346.

dedicauit...Concordiae aedem: The dedication, in 10 A. D., is recorded by the Fasti Praenestini: XVII. K. Feb. Concordiae Au*gustae aedis dedicata* est P. Dolabella C. Silano *cos.*: CIL I², p. 231. Another inscription, commemorating the restoration of the temple, though itself of somewhat later date, is generally believed to refer to the restoration undertaken by Tiberius: S. P. Q. R. | aedem Concordiae vetustate collapsam | inmeliorem (*sic*) faciem opere et cultu splendidiore restituit: CIL VI. 89. Five others dedicated to Concordia, four of them in behalf of the safety of Tiberius (cf. ad LIV), are likewise assigned to this period: CIL VI. 90–94.

XXI. 1.

lege...lata ut...cum Augusto...censum a[u]geret: Augustus duly names Tiberius as his assistant in holding this census in 14 A. D.: *tertiu*m consulari cum imperio lustrum | conlega Tib. Cae*sare filio feci* Sex. Pompeio et Sex. Appuleio cos.: Mon. Ancyr. 2. 8, 9, CIL III, p. 776. The only inscription that I know in which Tiberius is entitled *censor* is placed among the falsifications, though a few scholars deem it genuine: M. Plautius | M. f. Anien. | Lucanus, | Ti. Claudius | Ti. f. Pal. | Nero aed. cur., | pr., cens., II vir V...m. XIV v. v.....: CIL XIV. 361*.

XXIII.

Iure....tribuniciae potestatis: That Tiberius's tribunician power was continuous after his adoption by Augustus in 4 A. D., is evident from a fragment of the Fasti Cos. Capitolini, which includes the years 5–13, and names Tiberius with the proper tribunician date for each year as follows: e. g., 5 A. D., Ti. Caesar Augusti f., divi n., tribun. potest. VI : CIL I², p. 29.

atrox fortuna Gaium et Lucium filios mihi eripuit: Almost the same wording is used in Augustus's account of his reign: *filios* meos, quos iuv*enes m*ihi eripuit *fortuna, G*aium et Lucium Caesares: Mon. Ancyr. 2. 46, CIL III, p. 776.

XXV. 2.

Germaniciani...Germanicum, qui tum iis praeerat... urgebant: In this campaign Germanicus recovered the standards that had been lost by Varus in 9 A. D., in token of which victory a coin was struck with the following inscription: Germanicus Caesar, signis recept. devictis Germ. s. c.: Cohen 1, p. 225. 7. The very fragmentary inscription from the arch of Tiberius, in which the letters RECIP are preserved, probably refers to the same victory: CIL VI. 906; cf. Tac. *Ann.* 2.41.1. A number of inscriptions of slaves also bear witness to the German campaign, e. g.: Macro | Germaniciano | Ti. Caesaris | Germano | natione Vein.: CIL VI. 4339; cf. also 4336, 4337, 4341, 4344, 4351, 4357, 4398, all from Rome.

XXV. 3.

Libonem...secundo...anno in senatu coarguit: Cf. XXV. 1. This action in the senate is recorded in the Fasti Amiternini as follows: fer(iae) ex s(enatus) c(onsulto) q(uod) e(o) d(ie) | nefaria con|silia, quae de | salute Ti. Caes. liberorumq(ue) eius et | aliorum principum civi|tatis deq(ue) r(e) p(ublica) | inita ab | M. Libone erant, | in senatu | convicta | sunt: CIL I², p. 244 = IX. 4192. Since epigraphic evidence may, as a rule, be considered more trustworthy than literary, it seems probable that Suetonius is wrong in calling Libo *Lucius,* although Dio 57. 15 gives him the same praenomen.

XXVI. 1.

natalem suum...uix...honorari passus est: The Antian calendar shows that Tiberius's birthday fell within the period of the celebration in the Circus: XVI. K. Dec. in Circ. Ti. Aug. natal.: CIL I², p. 249; cf. Comm. Diurni, p. 335. That the day did receive recognition is evident from at least two inscriptions, one the Acts of the Arval Brothers: idem pro magistro ex decreto consulum (?) ob natalem | Ti. Caesaris divi Augusti f. Augusti, pontificis maximi, | tribunic. potestate XXXVII, cos. V, I(ovi) O(ptimo) M(aximo) b(ovem) m(arem) | immolavit: CIL VI. 2025 a; the other from Forum Clodi in Etruria for the year 18 A. D.: Ti. Caesare tert. Germanico Caesare iter. cos., | Cn. Acceio Cn. f. Arn(iensi tribu) Rufo Lutatio, T. Petillio P. f. Qui(rina tribu) II vir., | decreta: | .... natali Ti. Caesaris perpetue acturi decuriones | et populus cenarent — quam inpensam Q. Cascellio Labeone | in perpetuo. pollicenti, ut gratiae agerentur munificentiae eius — eoque | natali ut quotannis vitulus inmolaretur. | et ut natalibus Augusti et Ti. Caesarum, priusquam ad vescendum | decuriones irent, thure et vino genii eorum ad epulandum ara | numinis Augusti invitarentur: CIL XI. 3303.

templa, flamines, sacerdotes decerni sibi prohibuit: In spite of this prohibition there are a number of inscriptions of temples, flamens, seviri, and priests of Tiberius, none, however, occurring in Rome. A Greek inscription from Cyprus names a priest of the temple of Tiberius (IGR 3. 933), and a Latin one from the province of Byzacena is thought by Furneaux (I, p. 535) to have belonged either to a temple or to an altar: Romae et Imp. Ti. Caesari | Augusto sacrum | ||||||| : CIL VIII. 685. CIL II. 49 from Lusitania, IX. 652 from Lavello, X. 688 from Surrentum are each dedicated to a flamen of Tiberius. CIL IX. 6415 from Asculum, XI. 3781 from Veii, Dessau 6565 from Asculum are dedicated to, or mention, seviri of Tiberius. IGR 3.474 from Lycia, 1344 from Arabia, 1473 from Galatia, 4.256, 257 both from Assus, 454 from Pergamum, CIG 2943 from Nysa, each name a priest of Tiberius, the latter two even before he was adopted by Augustus. Fougères[1] believes that the cult of Tiberius existed in Lycia before it was made a province, and that it remained as a separate worship even after the cult of the Augusti was inaugurated in the province.

(prohibuit)...statuas atque imagines nisi permittente se poni: There is epigraphical evidence for several statues

---

[1] G. Fougères, *De Lyciorum communi*, Paris, 1898, p. 105.

dedicated to Tiberius, though whether with or without his per-
mission we cannot say: dedicatione statuarum Caesarum et
Augustae mulsum et crustla | pecunia nostra decurionib. et
populo dedimus, perpetuoque eius die | dedicationis daturo.
nos testati sumus, quem diem quo frequentior quod|annis sit,
servabimus VI. Idus Martias, qua die | Ti. Caesar pontif.
maximus felicissime est creatus: CIL XI. 3303 (18 A. D. from
Etruria, cf. supra ad *natalem* etc.); also CIL X. 7257. 19–23 from
Mt. Eryx, XIII. 1769 from Lugdunum, IGR 3. 157 from Ancyra,
in the Augusteum together with the Mon. Ancyr., 933 from
Cyprus.

Various other inscriptions, especially from the eastern prov-
inces, seem to indicate the deification of Tiberius, e. g.: *numini*
ac providentiae | *Ti. Caesar.* Aug. et senatus | eius die qui fuit
XV. K. Novembr. | Viriasius Naso procos. tertio sua pecunia |
consecravit: CIL III. 12036 from Crete; also II. 1516 from
Baetica. Of the inscription on the obelisk brought by Gaius
from Egypt, placed in his gardens on the Vatican, and now
standing in front of St. Peter's, Mommsen says that one could
not easily find another example of such a consecration made
to a man who had died and had not been enrolled among the
gods: divo Caesari divi Iulii f. Augusto | Ti. Caesari divi Augusti
f. Augusto | sacrum: CIL VI. 882. And the following Greek
inscriptions are some in which Tiberius is called Θεός: IGR 1.853
from Oczakow, 3. 715, 720, 721 all from Lycia, 933 from Cyprus,
4. 71 from Mytilene, 144 from Cyzicus (in which he is called the
greatest of the gods), 1144 from Lindus.

XXVI. 2.

praenomen...imperatoris recusauit: Although Tiberius
did decline this forename, there are many inscriptions, particularly Greek, in which it appears, none, it is true, from the City
itself: Imp. Ti. Caesari divi Aug. f. Aug., pontif. maximo, tri-
bunic. potest. XXXVIII, cos. V, | L. Manilius L. f. Arn. Bucco
II vir dedicavit (36 A. D.): Rev. Arch. 23 (1914), p. 488; also
CIL III. 8512 (26 A. D.) from Dalmatia, 10918 from Upper
Pannonia; VIII. 685 (cf. ad *templa* etc. XXVI. 1), 5205 from
proconsular Numidia, 10018, 10023, 10492 (?) all from Africa;
Eph. Ep. 5. 1336; 8, p. 462. 219; and the following Greek in-

scriptions: Αὐτοκράτορος | Τιβερίου Καίσαρος Σεβαστοῦ: Curtius u. Adler 221. 1, 2; also IGR 1. 659 from Lower Moesia, 853 from Oczakow (4-14 A. D.), 1164 (32-38 A. D.), 1166 both from Egypt; 3. 845 from Cilicia; 4. 10, 11 both from Eresus, 71, 72, 75 all from Mytilene, 137 from Cyzicus, 1288 from Monghla.

cognomen...patris patriae...(recusauit): There is a coin on which this surname of Tiberius appears: Ti. Caesar divi Aug. f., pater patriae: Cohen 1, p. 193. 42. But in view of Suetonius's statement and of Tac. *Ann.* 1. 72. 2, there does not seem to be sufficient justification for conferring the title upon Tiberius in the emendations of the Acta Arvalium, CIL VI. 2024. 5, 11, f. 13; 2026. 3. Dennison (p. 62) is wrong in mentioning CIG 2087 (= IGR 1. 853) as an inscription in which Tiberius is called *pater patriae*, for the title clearly belongs to Augustus: Αὐτοκράτορι Καίσαρι θεῷ θεοῦ υἱῷ Σε|βαστῷ, ἀρχιερεῖ μεγίστῳ, πατρὶ πατρίδος καὶ τοῦ σύμπαντος ἀ[νθρ]ώπων γένους, | καὶ Αὐτοκράτορι Σεβαστῷ θεοῦ υἱῷ Τι|βερίῳ Καίσαρι καὶ τῷ δήμῳ ῎Αβαβος| Καλλισθένους ἐκ τῶν ἰδίων ἀνέθη|κε τὴν στοάν.

ne Augusti quidem nomen...epistulis addidit: But the title *Augustus* is very common in inscriptions of Tiberius: v. passim.

nec amplius quam mox tres consulatus, unum paucis diebus....gessit: There is epigraphic evidence for Tiberius's third consulship (18 A. D.) in the inscription of Scirtus, a charioteer for the white faction: Ti. Caesare III Germanico Caesar. II cos.: CIL I², p. 73 = VI. 10051; also CIL IV. 1885 from Pompeii; VI. 1985 from Rome; XI. 1356 from Luna, 3303 from Forum Clodi. CIL I², p. 72 = X. 6639, from Antium, also names Tiberius and Germanicus as consuls, at the same time giving the name of the consul, Tubero, elected to take the place of Tiberius after he had withdrawn. At least two inscriptions of that year bear the names of Germanicus and Tubero as consuls: Cereri August. | matri agr. | L. Bennius Primus | mag. pagi | Bennia Primigenia | magistra fecer. | Germanico Caesare II | L. Seio Tuberone cos. | dies sacrifici XIII. K. Mai: CIL XI. 3196 from Nepet; also IX. 3664 from Marruvium.

alterum tribus mensibus: Only two inscriptions noting this fourth consulship of Tiberius (21 A. D.) seem to have survived—one, the same inscription of Scirtus mentioned above:

Ti. Caesare IIII Druso Caesar. II cos.: CIL I², p. 73; the other, a fragment of the Acta Arvalium, CIL VI. 32340.

tertium absens usque in Idus Maias: Besides the coin mentioned under LXV.1 (q. v. in connection with this passage), there is, so far as I know, only one inscription, from Nola, naming the consuls for 31 A. D., Tiberius's fifth consulship, and in that the name of Sejanus, his colleague, has been erased: Ti. Caesar Aug. V cos. !!!!!!!!!!!!! | suf. VII. Id. Mai Faustus Cornelius Sulla Sex. Teidius Catull. cos., | suf. K. Iul. L. Fulcinius Trio cos., | suf. K. Oct. P. Memmius Regulus cos.: CIL X. 1233.   On a broken amphora found in the ditch of the agger near the castra Praetoria appears the name of Tiberius as consul for the fifth time: Ti. Caesare V cos. | Gaditanum: CIL XV. 4570; and also in an inscription from the City which gives perhaps as full information on Tiberius's offices and titles as any (36 A. D.): Ti. Caesari divi | Augusti f., divi Iuli | nepoti Aug., pontifici | maximo, cos. V, | imp. VIII, tr. pot. XXXVIII, | auguri, XV vir. sacr. | faciend., VII vir. epulon. | L. Scribonius L. f. Vot. Celer | aedil. ex d(ecreto) d(ecurionum) | pro ludis: CIL VI. 903.

XXVII.

consularem....satisfacientem   sibi....suffugerit: Cf. XXIX.

XXIX.

Q. Haterio: This man is, according to Tac. *Ann.* I. 13, the ex-consul alluded to in XXVII. We have one fragmentary inscription of him: Q. Haterius... | sortit., tr. pl., pr., VII *vir epulonum*...; CIL VI. 1426; and two from the columbarium of his slaves: Hateria | Dorchas | sibi et | Primo | Q. Hateri Cellario | viro suo et patrono emit d(e) s(uo): CIL VI. 9251; also 9252.

XXX.

conseruatis senatui...maiestate pristina et potestate: The attitude of Tiberius toward the senate is portrayed in the speech of Claudius on the question of giving the Gauls the right of holding offices (48 A. D.), which was found on a bronze tablet in the province of Lugdunum: sane | novo *more* et divus Aug*ustus* avon*culus m*eus et patruus Ti. | Caesar omnem florem ubique coloniarum ac municipiorum, bo|norum scilicet virorum et locupletium, in hac curia esse voluit: CIL XIII. 1668. II. 2–4. Freedom of government might have been thought still to exist so long as Tiberius merely recommended men to the senate for office, as was the case recorded in an inscription from Allifae, now rather fragmentary: ....viacure | ...*tr. pl.*, pr., leg. | *imp.* Caesaris Augusti | *iter.*, per commendation. | Ti. Caesaris Augusti | ab senatu cos. dest. | .....patrono: CIL IX. 2342.

XXXI. 2.

Cetera....per magistratus...agebantur: That magistrates in goodly numbers did exist and even flourish under Tiberius seems evident from the numerous inscriptions of them that have survived,—a circumstance from which it seems not unreasonable to conclude that their position was probably just about the same as under Augustus and the republic. Of *praefecti quinquennales* of Tiberius there are at least three inscriptions: CIL IX. 4122 from the country of the Aequiculi, X. 5393 from Aquinum, 6101 from Formiae; of *procuratores*, two: CIL X. 7489 from Lipara, XII. 5842 from the state of the Vocontii; of *praefecti castrorum*, one: CIL X. 4868 from Venafrum; of *legati*, seven: CIL V. 2823 from Patavium (also *leg. pro pr.* of Tiberius), 4329 from Brixia; VI. 879 from Rome (*leg. pro pr.*); IX. 5645 from Trea; X. 5182 from Casinum; XIV. 3598 from Tibur; IGR 3.522 from Lycia (of Sextus Marcius Priscus, *legatus* of Vespasian and of all the emperors from Tiberius); of *quaestores* of Tiberius, five: CIL II. 3837 from Saguntum; XIV. 2802 from Gabii, 3607, 3608 both from Tibur; IGR 3.703 from Lycia; one *praefectus fabrum* of Tiberius, from Mogantiacum: CIL XIII. 6816; one *aequator monetae*, a slave of Tiberius, from Lugdunum: CIL XIII. 1820; and one from Sestinum of a man who, when appointed to Egypt by Tiberius in a judicial capacity, died in Aquitania: L. Voluseno | L. f. Clu(stumina tribu) Clementi | trib. mil., praef. | equit., praef. tir. | Gall. N*arbonen?* | sis... | *censum?* | accepit missus a | divo Aug.; hic cum | mitteretur a Ti. Caes. Aug. | in Aegypt. ad iur. dict., | decessit provinc. | Aquitania: CIL XI. 6011.

XXXII. 1.

de tribuendis...militaribus donis: A number of inscriptions record the presentation of military gifts by Tiberius. From

Dalmatia there are three: one of a certain Cornelius presented with a golden wreath and a spear without an iron head, CIL III. 2018; one of Marcus Vireius Celer, presented with a necklace, bracelets and breast ornaments, CIL III. 2718; one dedicated to Janus by a soldier whom Tiberius had presented with a necklace: Iano patri | Aug. sacrum | C. Iulius C. f. Ser(gia tribu) | Aetor aed., | donatus ab Ti. Caes. | Aug. f. Augusto torq. | maiore bello Delma|tico, ob honorem | IIviratus cum liberis | suis posuit: CIL III. 3158 (on the Dalmatian War, cf. IX. 2). Lucius Antonius Quadratus of the twentieth legion was presented with necklaces and bracelets: CIL V. 4365 from Brixia; and Marcus Vergilius Lusius with two spears without iron heads, and with golden wreaths by both Augustus and Tiberius: CIL. X. 4862 from Venafrum; cf. also XII. 2430(?) from Gallia Narbonensis.

quasi non omnium tribuendorum ipsi (consulares) ius haberent: An inscription from Africa shows that the ex-consuls evidently had the right, too, of levying in their provinces: L. Flaminius L. f. Arn(iensi tribu), | mil. leg. III Aug. | Ɣ Iuli Long*i* dilecto | lectus ab M. Silano mil. | annis XIX in praesidio | ut esset in saltu Philomu|siano; ab hostem (*sic*) in pugna | occisus, vixit pie | annis XL | h(ic) s(itus) e(st): CIL VIII. 14603.

XXXIII.

Paulatim principem exeruit: There are two inscriptions which may, perhaps, be illustrative of Tiberius's gradually increasing show of authority. Under XXX is quoted an inscription of a man merely recommended for office. From Brixia we have one, rather fragmentary, of a man chosen by a decree of the senate and *by the authority of Tiberius Caesar*, CIL V. 4348; while from Aquinum there is one of a man chosen as patron of the colony *by the authority and permission of Tiberius:* Q. Decio Q. f., M. n. | Saturnino | pontif. minori Romae, tubi-cini | sacror. publ. p. R. quirit., praef. fabr., cos. | ter, curatori viarum Labic. | et Latinae, | trib. mil., praef. fabr. i. d. et sor-tiend. | iudicibus in Asia, | IIII vir. i. d. Veronae, | q. bis, II vir. i. d., II vir. iter., quinq., praef. | quinq. Ti. Caesaris Augusti iter., | Drusi Caesaris Ti. f. tertio, Neronis | Caesaris Germanici f., pontif., flamini | Romae et divi August. perpetuo, ex auctor. |

Ti. Caesaris Augusti et permissu *e*ius | cooptato coloniae patrono, | publice d. d.: CIL X. 5393.

XXXV. 2.

sub Kal. Iul.....conduceret: In the one inscription that I have found concerning renting of houses, the date named is the Ides of July, but it has been emended to the Kalends, on the strength, partly, of this passage in Suetonius: insula Arriana | Polliana Cn. Al*l*ei Nigidi Mai | locantur ex *K.* Iulis primis tabernae | cum pergulis suis et cenacula | equestria, et domus conductor | convenito primum Cn. Al*l*ei | Nigidi Mai ser.: CIL IV. 138 from Pompeii. Cic. *Ad Q. fr.* 2.3.7, *Ep.* 13.2; Mart. 12. 32.1; and Petron. 38 also mention the Kalends of July as moving day, or the day for renting houses.

XXXVI.

externas caerimonias, Aegyptios Iudaicosque ritus compescuit: As pontifex maximus the emperor had a free hand in regulating forms of religious worship and in determining the gods who should be recipients of that worship. That Tiberius held that office is evident from many inscriptions,—from the calendars, which record the date of his attaining to it, Mar. 10, 15 A. D.: *VI.* Id. Mart. feriae ex s. c. q(uod) *e*(*o*) d(*ie*) Ti. Caesar pontifex max. fac. est Druso et | Norbano *cos.*: Fasti Praen., CIL I², p. 233, cf. Fasti Vaticani, CIL VI. 2299, and CIL XI. 3303 fin. (quoted under XXVI. 1 prohibuit statuas etc.); and from the numerous inscriptions in which the title is affixed to his name, e. g.: Tib. Caesar divi | Augusti f. Augustus, | pont. max., imp., trib. | potest. XVIII, cos. desig. tert.: CIL III. 2972 from Dalmatia; also XIV. 2911 from Praeneste.

That the earlier cults, both Roman and Greek, still lived, is evident from inscriptions honoring the old gods, e. g. on a stone altar in the land of the Petrucorii,: Iovi O. M. et | Genio | Ti. Augusti | sacrum, | laniones: CIL XIII. 941; also of Jupiter, CIL XIII. 3026 a. 1. from Lutetia Parisiorum; of Janus, one from Dalmatia, quoted under XXXII. 1 (CIL III. 3158); of the Olympian Zeus, for the safety of Tiberius and Livia, IGR 3. 1344 from Arabia; of Cronos, from Egypt, 32 A. D., dedicated, however, by a suppliant (or priest = προστάτης) of Isis; IGR 1. 1172 of Apollo, from Egypt, 24 A. D., IGR. 1. 1320; of

Aphrodite, from her temple in Paphos, IGR 3. 941 (15 A. D.), 942; of Pluto from Galatia, IGR 3. 1473; of Hermes, from Egypt, IGR 1. 1362 (33 A. D.), 1365 (35 A. D.), 1366 (27/28 A. D.); of Pan, also all from Egypt, IGR 1. 1237 (20 A. D.), 1239 (29 A. D.), 1240 (30 A. D.), the last two being dedicated also to the gods having the same temple with Pan. But there are also several from Egypt honoring Egyptian deities, from which it may be concluded, that even if Tiberius drove Egyptian rites from Rome, he did not attempt to suppress them outside of Rome: of Isis there is one from 23 A. D., IGR 1. 1309; of Isis, Harpocrates and Pan, "the greatest gods," one from 21/22 A. D., IGR 1. 1171; of Serapis, one from 20/21 A. D., IGR 1. 1051; and of Thermouthis,[1] one from 25 A. D., IGR 1. 1084.

XXXVII. 3.

Cottl regno: On an arch at Segusio there is an inscription to Augustus, in which are named the peoples that comprised the kingdom of Cottius: Imp. Caesari Augusto divi f., pontifici maxumo, tribunic. potestate XV, imp. XIII, | M. Iulius Regis Donni f. Cottius praefectus ceivitatium quae subscriptae sunt: Segoviorum, Segusinorum, | Belacorum, Caturigum, Medullorum, Tebaviorum, Adanatium, Savincatium, Ecdiniorum, Veaminiorum, | Venisamorum, Iemeriorum, Vesubianiorum, Quadiatium, et ceivitates quae sub eo praefecto fuerunt: CIL V. 7231. Two inscriptions of freedmen of Cottius also have survived: CIL V. 7262 (?), 7296, both from Segusio.

aboleuit et ius moremque asylorum: In connection with this there is an interesting inscription from Nysa (mentioned ad XXVI. 1), which notes the restoration of records concerning the gods and the right of asylum: multa... Ἀρτεμίδωρος Δημητρίου,... ἐπιμεληθεὶς ἀποκατέστη|σεν εἰς῾τὸ γραμματ[εῖ]ον τὰ ἱερὰ γράμματα περὶ τῶν θεῶν|καὶ τῆς ἀσυλίας αὐτ[ῶ]ν καὶ τῆ[ς] ἱκεσίας καὶ τῆς περὶ τὸ ἱε|ρὸν ἀτ[ε]λ[εί]ας etc. : CIG 2943.

Cyzicenis...libertatem ademit: Though there is no inscription from Cyzicus referring to this particular incident, there are three of interest in connection with Tiberius: one (mentioned ad XXVI. 2), a simple dedication giving merely Tiberius's name, IGR 4. 137; another recording the respect

---

[1] Cf. W. Spiegelberg, *Aegypt. u. griech. Eigennamen,* Leipzig, 1901, pp. 12* ff.

shown to Tiberius and his family by Antonia Tryphaena, the daughter of royal parentage, and her dedication to Athena Polias of a statue of Livia, termed Νεικηφόρος, the epithet of the goddess herself, bestowed because of the great help given by Athena to the people of Cyzicus in the Mithridatic war,[1] IGR 4. 144; the third, on an honorary arch erected jointly to Augustus, Tiberius and Claudius by the Roman citizens at Cyzicus and the inhabitants of Cyzicus: divo Aug. Caesari, Ti. Aug. *divi Aug. f.* | imp., Ti. Claudio Drusi f. *Caesari Aug. Ger*|manico pont. max., *tr. p. XI, cos. V, imp. XXI,* | p. p., vind. lib., devi*ctori regum XI* | Britanniae, ar*cum posuerunt* | c. R. qui Cyzici *consistunt* | et Cyzicen*i* | curatore...: CIL III. 7061.

XXXVII. 4.

Archelaum Cappadocem: Cf. VIII.

XXXIX.

Germanicus in Syria...**(obierat):** The Fasti Antiates mark Oct. 10 as Infer. Germanic. (CIL I², p. 249), which may, therefore, have been the day of his death; and, in fact, being so interpreted, it has caused the following restoration in the Ostian calendar: *inferiae actae ob excessum* Germanici: CIL XIV. 244. A number of inscriptions from the East, dedicated to Germanicus, are probably due to his having been in Asia Minor: CIL III. 334 from Apamea, 426 from Ephesus; IGR 3. 715 from Lycia, 4. 11 from Eresus, 326 and 327 from Pergamum, 979 from Samos.

Drusus Romae obierat: We have an honorary tablet dedicated to Drusus by the plebs of the city, probably after his death: plebs urbana quinque et | triginta tribuum | Druso Caesari Ti. Aug. f., | divi Augusti n., | divi Iulii pronepoti, | pontifici, auguri, sodal. Augustal., | cos. iterum, tribunic. potest. iter., | aere conlato: CIL VI. 910; also the fragments of a senatusconsultum decreeing honors to Drusus after his death: CIL VI. 912. In CIL XII. 3180, 3207, both from Nemausus, and in Curtius u. Adler 372, Germanicus and Drusus are associated, the first two inscriptions being dedicated each to a flamen of both Germanicus and Drusus, the third recording the honor

---

[1] K. J. Marquardt, *Cyzicus*, Berlin, 1836, p. 132.

paid them both by the city of the Eleans and the Olympic Council. CIL II. 194 from Lusitania, XII. 1872 from Vienna (Vienne on the Rhone), are each dedicated to a flamen of Germanicus.

XL.

cum...Nolae templum Augusti...dedicasset: The flamen of Augustus to whom the following inscription from Nola is dedicated, was, perhaps, connected with this temple: L. Curiatio L. f. | flamini divi Augusti, | prim. pil., trib. milit. II, | praef. castr., praef. fabr., | arbitratu Hyacinthi lib.: CIL X. 1262.

Capreas se contulit: A few inscriptions of home-born slaves from Capri have been preserved, which are believed to belong to members of Tiberius's household on that island: Iunoni | Dorcadis | Iuliae Augustae l. vernae Caprensis | ornatricis | Lycastus conlibertus | rogator coniugi | carissimae sibi: CIL VI. 8958; also VI. 8409 a, X. 6638. C. 3. 3.

XLI.

ut...Moesiam...uastari neglexerit: Yet two inscriptions from Moesia tell us that two legions were stationed there, confirming the statement in Tac. *Ann.* 4. 5. 5: Ti. Caesare Aug. f. | Augusto imperator., | pont. max., tr. pot. XXXV. | leg. IIII Scyt., leg. V. Maced.: CIL III. 1698; cf. also 13813 b.

XLII. 1.

Pomponio Flacco: The name of Pomponius, who was consul in 17 A. D., together with that of his colleague, C. Caelius Rufus, appears in several inscriptions,—in the Fasti Arvalium, CIL I², p. 70; the Fasti Ant., CIL I², p. 72; the inscription of Scirtus, CIL I², p. 73; and in the Fasti Lunenses, where, however, we read L. Pontio Flacco C. Caecilio cos.: CIL I², p. 73.

L. Pisone: His name occurs a number of times in the Acta Arvalium, CIL VI. 2023 a. 7, 14, 23; 2024. 2, 32; 32340; also in the Fasti Colotiani as consul for B. C. 15, together with Marcus Livius Drusus, CIL I², p. 64; and in an inscription from Veleia, CIL XI. 1182. The following inscription of a slave of Lucius Piso may belong either to one of his slaves, or to one of those of the Piso who was consul in 57 A. D.: Iulla | L. Pisonis pontif. Aemilia Helpis | merenti fecit: CIL VI. 20743; cf. Ephem. Ep. 1, pp. 148, 149.

XLII. 2.

Cestio Gall[i]o: His name, together with that of his colleague, M. Servilius Nonianus, as consuls for the year 35 A. D., appears in an inscription from Rome, Notizie degli Scavi 1894, p. 280, and in another from Sicily, IGR 1. 495 (the form *Cestius* rather than *Sestius*, which some manuscripts give, being confirmed by the Greek transliteration Κέστιος).

XLVII.

Princeps neque opera ulla magnifica fecit: But many inscriptions are evidence that Tiberius, as emperor, was not neglectful of all public needs and desires. A bridge at Vaga was given by him in 29 A. D.: Ti. Caesar divi | Aug. f. Augustus | pontif. max., trib. | potest. XXXI, cos. IIII | dedit, | C. Vibius Marsus pr. | cos. III dedica.: CIL VIII. 10568; another at Arminium given, according to the inscription, by both Augustus and Tiberius, was probably begun by Augustus and finished by Tiberius in 20 A. D., CIL XI. 367; another over the Tagus near Garovilla was probably given by Tiberius in 25 A. D.: CIL II. 4651. At Brixia Augustus and Tiberius built an aqueduct, CIL V. 4307; at Nicopolis, in Syria, Tiberius alone built one between 21 and 30 A. D., CIL III. 6703; while in Rome three inscriptions from the Aqua Virgo, and a fourth not definitely assigned, probably testify to reconstruction under Tiberius: Virg. | Ti. Caesar Aug. | pontif. maxim., | trib. pot. XXXVIII, | cos. V, imp. VIII, | IIII, | p. CCXL: CIL VI. 1253 b; also 1253 a (cf. 31565 a, c), 1255 (cf. 31571), Rev. Arch. 18 (1911), p. 509. 177. In Veii in 28 A. D. Tiberius gave a portico, CIL XI. 3784; in 27 he presented something not revealed because of the fragmentary condition of the inscription, CIL XI. 3783; the gift of Augustus and Tiberius in Emona, in Pannonia, 14 A. D., is also unknown for the same reason, CIL III. 10768. A very large number of inscriptions refer to Tiberius's restoring and rebuilding of roads: CIL II. 4904, 4905 from Spain; VIII. 10023 from Africa; and from Gallia Narbonensis, CIL XII. 5441, 5445, 5449, 5478, 5492, 5554, 5557, 5588, 5592, 5596, 5598, 5600, 5605, 5606, 5619, 5628, 5638, 5649, 5652, 5654, 5657, 5659, 5665; from Latium, CIL XIV. 4086. In the Carcer at Rome there is an inscription recording a restoration, assigned usually to Tiberius's reign: C. Vibius C. f. Rufinus M. Cocceius

M. f. Nerva cos. ex s(enatus) c(onsulto): CIL VI. 1539. The name of Tiberius on a number of water pipes may indicate his influence in civic improvement, or may simply date the work: CIL X. 1897 a from Puteoli; XV. 7266, 7267, 7268, 7814, 7815, all from Rome.   Two other inscriptions record gifts of Tiberius, both however, before he was emperor: *Ti. Claudius Ti. f.* | Nero cos. templa, porticus, | hortos municipio dedit: CIL V. 2149 from Altinum; also CIL V. 6358 from Laus Pompeia.

XLVIII.1.

Publice munificentiam bis omnino exhibuit: Suetonius ignores Tiberius's act of munificence after the fire in 36 A. D., which destroyed part of the Circus and the Aventine.   Tacitus, however, mentions it (*Ann.* 6. 45), and a fragment of the Fasti recently discovered at Ostia, records the same occurrence: K. Nov. Pars Circi inter|ultores arsit ad quod T*i*. Caesar IIS | $\overline{\infty}$ | public*e d.*: Notizie degli Scavi vol. XIV (1917), p. 182.

XLVIII. 2.

missiones ueteranorum rarissimas fecit: We have one inscription from Nemausus of a soldier of Tiberius who received his discharge after 25 years of service: Ti. Caesaris | divi Aug. f. Augusti | miles missicius, T. Iulius | Festus, militavit annos XXV | in legione XVI, decreto decurion. | accepit frumenti m(odios) L, balneum et | sui gratuitum in perp. et aream in|ter duos turres per P. Pusonium Pere|grinum IIII vir. et XI vir. adsignatam: CIL XII. 3179.   Other inscriptions show that 25 or 26 years of service was not unusual, while a few from Dalmatia testify to even more than 30 years: CIL III. 2014 (33 years), 2048 (32 years), 2818 (38 years), 2834 (43 years).   Since the soldiers named in 2014 and 2834 belonged respectively to the seventh and eleventh legions called Claudia Pia Fidelis, we know that they ended their service under Claudius, though the greater part of their terms must necessarily have been under Tiberius. The last man, Mommsen thinks, served voluntarily (cf. CIL III, p. 282).

Asia…ciuitatibus: The liberality shown by Tiberius on this occasion is noted in several inscriptions that have come down to us: Ti. Caesari divi | Augusti f., divi | Iuli n. Augusto | pontif. maximo, cos. IIII, | imp. VIII, trib. potestat. XXXII, |

Augustales. | respublica | restituit. | *Eu*thenia Sard*es* Ulloron, *Magnes*ia, | Philadelphea, Tmolus, Cyme, | *T*emnos, Cibyra, Myrina, Ephesos, Apollonidea, Hyrca*n*ia, | Mostene, *A*egae, *Hiero*caesarea: CIL X. 1642 = Rushforth p. 123, from Puteoli. From Aegae there is a rather fragmentary one: *Ti. Caesar divi Aug. f., divi Iuli n. Aug. imp., p.* m., tr. p., *cos.* V, conditor uno tem*pore XII civitatium t*errae motu ve*xatarum:* CIL III. 7096; while from Hadjiléri there is one in Greek with almost the same wording, Dessau 8785 = Bull. de Coresp. Hell. 1887, p. 90 = IGR 4. 1351. Two Greek inscriptions from Cibyra also refer to the help given by Tiberius as the "founding" (κτίσις) of the city: IGR 4. 914, 915. And in commemoration of the event a coin was struck, bearing a picture of the colossal statue that was dedicated to Tiberius, and also the following inscription: Ti. Caesar divi Aug. f. August. p. m., tr. pot. XXIII, s. c. civitatibus Asiae restitutis: Cohen 1, p. 189. 3.

XLIX. 1.

Cn. Lentulum Augurem: An inscription from Caria is dedicated to Lentulus as proconsul: [Γ]ν[αί]ῳ Λέντλῳ Αὔγουρι τῷ ἀνθυπά|τῳ: CIG 2943. 12, 15. His name appears several times in the Acta Arvalium: CIL VI. 2023 a. 1, 10, 19; also together with that of his colleague in the consulship 14 B. C., Marcus Licinius Crassus, in the Fasti Biondiani, CIL I². p. 65; on one of the tesserae consulares, CIL I¹. 745; on a tile, CIL I¹. 797 = XI. 6673. 21; in a sepulchral inscription from Rome, CIL VI. 23532; in two inscriptions from Pompeii, CIL X. 885, 886; on a lead jar from Puteoli, CIL X. 1938. One of his freedmen is named in an inscription from Sulmo, CIL IX. 3099.

Quirini consularis: The several inscriptions of this man favor the form *Quirinius* rather than *Quirinus*, as do also Tac. *Ann.* 2. 30; 3. 22, 48; Strab. 12. 6. 5; Jos. *Ant.* 18. 1. 1; St. Luke 2. 2. A rather fragmentary inscription from Tibur has been assigned to Quirinius by Mommsen: *P. Sulpicius P. f. Quirinius cos. . . . . ; proconsul Cretam et Cyrenas provinciam optinuit . . . . ; legatus pr. pr., divi Augusti Syriam et Phoenicen optinens bellum gessit cum gente Homonadensium quae interfecerat Amyntam r|egem, qua redacta in pot|estatem imp. Caesaris | Augusti populique Romani senatu|s dis immortalibus | supplicationes binas ob res prosp|ere gestas et | ipsi ornamenta triumph|alia*

decrevit; | pro consul. Asiam provinciam op|*tinuit; legatus pr. pr.* |
divi Augusti *i*terum Syriam et Ph*oe*nic*en* op*t*inuit: CIL XIV.
3613. An inscription from the province of Byzacena names
him together with Gaius Valgius, his colleague in the consulship 12 B. C., CIL VIII. 68; also X. 3804 from Capua; another
probably from Berytus calls him the governor of Caesar in
Syria, CIL III. 6687. 4.   At Antioch in 1912 Sir William Ram-
say found an inscription designating him as *duumvir,* and sub-
sequently wrote an article thereon entitled *Luke's Narrative
of the Birth of Christ,* The Expositor, 8th ser. (1912), vol. 4, pp.
385–407, 481–507. The inscription, to be dated probably 8
B. C., reads as follows: C. Carista*nio* | C. f. Ser. Front*oni* |
Caesiano Iulio, | praef. fabr., pon*tif.,* | sacerdoti, praefecto | P.
Sulpici Quirini duumviri, | praefecto M. Servili. | huic primo
omnium | publice d(ecurionum) d(ecreto) statua | posita est:
ib. p. 401.

L. 2.

matrem Liuiam . . . uindicantem: Numerous memorials
seem to indicate that Livia's importance in the eyes of the people
was not much inferior to that of Tiberius.   Following the terms
of Augustus's will (cf. *Aug.* CI. 2.), she assumed the name
Augusta, and as such appears in inscriptions practically on an
equality with Tiberius.   So there are dedications to both
together: Ti. Caesari divi | Aug. f. Augusto. | Iuliae Augustae |
divi Augusti: CIL VI. 3750 = 31277; also 905, both from
Rome; from Ancyra an inscription mentioning statues of them
both (cf. ad XXVI. 1), IGR 3. 157; and three Greek inscriptions in which they are together called Σεβαστοί, IGR 3.
312 from Galatia, 1086 from Syria, 1344 from Arabia.   A lead
pipe from Tusculum is inscribed as follows: *T*i. Caesaris et
Iuliae Augu*stae:* Ephem. Ep. 9, p. 417. 700; and in many inscriptions of their slaves or freedmen, they are named as joint
owners or patrons, e. g.: Prima Augusti | et Augustae l. | nutrix
Iuliae Germa|*nici* filiae: CIL VI. 4352; also 4173, 4358, 4770,
4776, 5181, 5215, 5223, 5226, 5248, 5316, 5745, 8656, 8913,
8989, 9066, 14843—all from the City.   The Fasti Praenestini
record the dedication of a statue to Augustus, noteworthy because of the order of the names, which, it is likely, followed
the original inscription; VIII. K. Mai sig(num) divo **Augusto**
patri ad theatrum Marc*ell.* | Iulia Augusta et Ti. **Augustus**
dedicarunt: CIL I², p. 236; cf. Tac. *Ann.* 3. 64.

ut titulis suis...**Liuiae filius adiceretur:** So far as I know, we have no inscriptions in which Tiberius is entitled "son of Livia," but there are many in which Livia is entitled "mother of Tiberius," e. g.: Iuliae August. divi | Augusti matri Ti. Cae|saris Aug. L. Volusio | Saturnino leg. pro pr. | C. Iulius C. f. Sulla *ob dec.:* CIL III. 9972 from Dalmatia; also CIL II. 2038 from Anticaria; IX. 3304 from Superaequum; X. 7340, 7501, both from Sicily; XI. 1165 from Veleia (wherein she is also styled daughter of Augustus, which she became by adoption in 14 A. D.); IGR 1. 1150 from Egypt; 3. 720 from Lycia; 4. 144 from Cyzicus. In two Greek inscriptions, however, Tiberius is called son of the Augusti: Τιβέριον Καίσαρα θεὸν Σεβαστὸν, | θεῶν Σεβαστῶν υἱὸν, αὐτοκ[ρ]άτορα | γῆς καὶ θαλάσσης, τὸν εὐεργέτην | καὶ σωτῆρα τοῦ σύνπαντος [κ]όσμου, | Μυρέων ὁ δῆμος: IGR 3. 721 from Lycia; also 4. 1144 from Lindus.

L. 3.

non parentem patriae appellari...**passus est:** Yet there are coins from Africa on which Livia is called *mater patriae:* Cohen 1, p. 165. 807, p. 207. 203; and *genetrix orbis* both on a coin and in an inscription: Iuliae Aug. Drusi *f.*, divi *Aug.*, | matri Ti. Caesaris Aug. principis | et conservatoris, et Drusi Ger|manici, gen*etrici* orbis, | M. Cornelius Proculus | pontufex Caesarum: CIL II. 2038; also Cohen 1, p. 169. 3, both from Baetica. Three other coins bear the head of Livia, one with the inscription Pietas, Drusus Caesar Ti. Augusti f., tr. pot. iter., s. c.: Cohen 1, p. 170. 1; the other two with Iustitia and Salus Augusta respectively, and Ti. Caesar divi Aug. p. m., tr. pot. XXIIII, s. c.: Cohen 1, p. 171. 4, 5. An inscription from Rome dedicated to Pietas Augusta is from an altar that was ordered in 22 A. D., at the time of Livia's illness, but not erected until 43, CIL VI. 562.

LI. 2.

prohibuit (Liuiam) consecrari: We know from *Claud.* XI. 2 that Livia was later officially deified; and while the majority of the inscriptions indicating her deification are therefore probably from the reign of Claudius or later, a few seem to show that in some parts of the empire she received this honor even during the reign of Tiberius, e. g.: *Ti.* Caesari divi Aug. f. Augusto, divae Augus*tae* | M. Iunius C. f. Gal. Proculus praef.

equit. divi Aug., fab(rum), sua pec. fec*it*. | Pompeia Q. f. Tre-
bulla testamento suo ex IIS C̄ refici iussit... : CIL X. 6309 from
Tarracina; also X. 7501 from Sicily, and, perhaps, an inscription from Rome of a freedwoman of Livia, VI. 1815, and from
Haluntium in Sicily, a dedication to Livia by the town, X. 7464.

LII. 2.

Iliensium legatis...consolantibus: It is interesting to
note the relations between Ilium and Tiberius. When in 26
A. D. eleven cities contested for the privilege of dedicating a
temple to Tiberius, Livia and the senate, and Smyrna was
granted the right (cf. Tac. *Ann.* 4. 15, 55), Ilium, one of the un-
successful candidates, nevertheless paid honor to the emperor,
as is evident from the following inscription, dedicated by the
council and the people in 32-33: Τιβέριον Καίσαρα θεοῦ Σεβαστοῦ
υἱὸν | Σεβαστὸν ἀρχιερέα δημαρχικῆς ἐξουσίας τὸ λγ́, ὕπατον τὸ έ, τὸν
συν|γενῆ καὶ σωτῆρα καὶ εὐεργέτην ἡ βουλὴ | καὶ ὁ δῆμος: IGR 4. 207.

quod (Germanicus)...Alexandream...se adisset: An
inscription dedicated to him has been found at Alexandria:
Germanico Caesari Ti. *Aug. f.* | L. Valerius | L. Tonneius le... |
A. Mevius... | magistri larum Aug. | anno V. Ti. Caes*aris Aug.*:
CIL III. 12047. In connection with Tiberius's attitude toward
Germanicus, it is notable that, although the Fasti Antiates and
the Ostienses record what is possibly the day of Germanicus's
death (cf. ad **XXXIX**), the Fasti Amiternini, written in Tiberius's reign, do not. Besides the many inscriptions of Germanicus
already noted (cf. ad **XV.** 2, **XXXIX**), a few particularly seem
to suggest the general goodwill toward him: plebs urbana
quinque et | triginta tribuum | Germanico Caesari | Ti. Augusti
f., | divi Augusti n., | auguri, flamini Augustali, | cos. iterum,
imp. iterum, | aere conlato: CIL VI. 909 from Rome, from which
also come the fragments of a senatusconsultum decreeing honors
to him after his death, CIL VI. 911; also, from Antium: Ger-
manico Caesari Ti. Caesaris f., divi Augusti n. | C. Iulius Chi-
marus; idem statuas et aediculam | refecit, sedes marmoreas
posuit: CIL X. 6649.

LII. 3.

Cn. Pisonem legatum Syriae: I have found no inscription
of him from Syria, but his name appears with that of Tiberius
as consuls for the year B. C. 7 (cf. ad **IX.** 3).

LIII. 1.

Nurum Agrippinam: A number of inscriptions, especially Greek, are dedicated to her or at least include her name, e. g.: Agrippinae M. f. | Germanici: CIL IX. 2635 from Aesernia; also CIL II. 3379 from Tarraconensis; VI. 31281 from Rome; XI. 1167 from Veleia; one from Lycia, calling her the grand-daughter of Augustus: Ἀγριπ[π]ε[ῖ]ναν [θ]υγατριδῆν | θεοῦ Σε[βαστ]οῦ Καίσαρος, | [γ]υναῖκα δ[ὲ Γ]ε[ρ]μαν[ιχ]οῦ | [Κ]αίσαρος, Μυρέων [ὁ δ]ῆμο[ς]: IGR 3. 716; cf., too, IGR 3. 94 from Paphlagonia; 4. 74, 75 both from Mytilene, 980 from Samos, 1300 from Aeolia; CIG 1301 from Messenia, 2183 from Mytilene; Bull. de corr. Hell. 4 (1880), p. 432. 17, 18 from Lesbos; Ath. Mitt. V (1880), p. 197 from Delphi; Jour. Hell. Stud. 17 (1897), p. 17, 39 from Melos; also Cohen 1, p. 231 sqq.

LIII. 2.

(eam) Pandatariam relegauit ... ita absumptam: In *Cal.* XV. 1 we read that Caligula brought his mother's bones from Pandataria to Rome, and an inscription on a marble urn from Rome verifies this statement: ossa | Agrippinae M. Agrippae f., | divi Aug. neptis, uxoris | Germanici Caesaris, | matris C. Caesaris Aug. | Germanici principis: CIL VI. 886.

LIV. 1.

Neronem: There are a number of inscriptions dedicated to him or mentioning him, e. g., one from Rome rather fully naming his offices: Neroni Caesari | Germanici Caesaris f., | Ti. Caesaris Augusti n., | divi Augusti pron., | flamini Augustali, | sodali Augustali, | sodali Titio, fratri Arvali, | fetiali, quaestori, | ex s. c.: CIL VI. 913; also one from Dalmatia dedicated by the cities of Liburnia, CIL III. 2808 (cf. 9879); V. 23 from Pola, 6416. 1 from Ticinum (in which the name of Tiberius as his grandfather is omitted, though Augustus, his great-grandfather, is named); VI. 31274 from Rome (dedicated also to his father Germanicus, and to his brother Drusus); X. 5393. 12 from Aquinum; XI. 3336 from Blera, 3789 from Veii; IGR 4. 74, 75 both from Mytilene, 1300 from Aeolia (both 74 and 1300 calling him simply the son of Germanicus and Agrippina, without mention of either Tiberius or Augustus).

Drusum: Of him, too, we have several inscriptions, e. g., from the Troad: Druso Caesari | Germanici Caesaris | filio, | Ti.

Augusti nepoti, | divi Augusti pronepoti, | pontifici | d. d.: CIL III. 380; from Bordeaux a fragmentary one in which he is entitled praefectus urbi, sodalis Augustalis, CIL XIII. 589; also V. 6416, 9 from Ticinum (without mention of Tiberius); VI. 31274 (cf. ad *Neronem*); XI. 3788 from Veii; XIV. 3607. 6 from Tibur; IGR 4. 75 from Mytilene (designating him as son of Germanicus and Agrippina).

Gaium: Besides the inscriptions of Gaius as emperor, there are several of the time prior to his accession, e. g. two from Vienna (Vienne on the Rhone): C. Caesari | Germanici f., | *Ti*. Augusti n., | divi Aug. pron. | Germanico | pontifici, q.: CIL XII. 1848, 1849; also, perhaps, IGR 4. 1001 from Aegiala, 1022 from Calymna.

Tiberium: There is an inscription of him from Alba Pompeia: Ti. Caesari | Drusi f., | Ti. August*i* n., | divi Augusti pron*ep*. | P. Varius P. f. Aem. | Ligus filius: CIL V. 7598. In another from near Salamis Tiberius is named together with his twin brother, Germanicus, who died when he was four years old: ...ἀρχιερέως] | διὰ βίου, αὐτοῦ [τε καὶ τῶν] | διδύμων υἱῶν Δ[ρούσου] | Τιβερίου καὶ Γερμανικο[ῦ], | γυμνασιάρχων τῶ[ν... : IGR 3. 997. Mommsen believes that a very fragmentary inscription from Brixia also refers to these twins sons of Drusus: *Liviae Drusi Caesaris, matri T*i. et *Germanici C*aesarum h.... : CIL V. 4311.

diem...utriusque tirocinii congiario...celebrauit: This statement is confirmed with respect to the day of Nero's attaining his majority (June 7, 20 A. D.), by the following record from Ostia: M. Valerius Messalla M. Au*relius Cotta cos*., | VII. Idus Iun. Nero to*gam virilem* | sumpsit; cong(iaria) di*visit*: CIL XIV. 244.

pro eorum...salute publice uota suscepta: I have found no record of such vows offered for their safety, but of those for the safety of Tiberius, a number survive, e. g., from Capena: Ti. Caesari divi Augusti f. | Augusto | pontif. maximo, cos. V, | trib. potest. XXXIIII, | principi optumo ac | iustissimo, conservatori | patriae, pro salute et | incolumitate eius | A. Fabius Fortunatus viator *cos*. | et pra*et*., | Augustalis prim*us*, | voto suscepto p.: CIL XI. 3872; from the temple of Concord in Rome: Q. Coelius L. f., pr., | aed. pl. cer., | pro pr. ex s. c., q., | ex voto suscepto | pro incolumitate | Ti. Caesaris divi Aug. f. | Augusti |

pontific. maxim., | Concordiae d. d. | *auri* p. XXV: CIL VI. 91;
also from Rome 92 (cf. 30690), 93, 94 (on these four cf. ad XX
fin.), 3675 (cf. 30856), the Acta Arvalium, 2025. 15 sqq. (recording the payment and renewal of a vow), 2027; from Aveia, CIL
IX. 3607. From Leuci comes an interesting inscription which
exemplifies, says Hirschfeld, the first use of the phrase *divinae
domus:* CIL XIII. 4635; cf. Phaedr. 5. 8. 38. CIL VI. 2024. 10
sqq. from Rome, IGR 3. 1086 from Syria are for the safety of
both Tiberius and Livia, CIL VI. 2026 for Tiberius, Livia and their
household; while in the Acta Arvalium, CIL VI. 32340, Tiberius,
Julia, and their household are simply included in a formal, com-
prehensive prayer for the good of the whole Roman people.

LIV. 2.

amborum...reliquias...uix...colligi possent: That the
bones of Nero were gathered and brought to Rome is known
from *Cal.* XV. 1, and from an inscription from Rome, in which
the omission of Tiberius's name is marked and intentional:
ossa | Neronis Caesaris | Germanici Caesaris f., | divi Aug. pron.,
flamin. | Augustalis, quaestoris: CIL VI. 887. If the bones of
Drusus were not gathered, an altar to his manes might appro-
priately be erected in any locality. So we have on an altar
from Camunni: dis manibus | Drusi Caesaris Germ*anici* f.:
CIL V. 4953.

LVII. 1.

fauorem hominum moderationis simulatione captaret:
There is a coin struck to honor, or perhaps to invite, moderation
on Tiberius's part: Ti. Caesar divi Aug. f. August. imp. VIII,
moderationi, s. c.: Cohen 1, p. 190. 5.

LXII. 1.

Liuillae uxoris (Drusi): In the surviving inscriptions of
her slaves and freedmen, all from Rome, she appears as *Livia*,
e. g.: M. Livius | Augustae lib. | Prytanis | Liviae Drusi paedag.:
CIL VI. 33787; Cyrus | Liviae Drusi Caes. | medicus: CIL VI
8899; also 4349, 15502, 19747, 20237. Cf. CIL V. 4311 ad
Tiberium LIV. 1.

LXIII. 1.

(Tiberius) inuisus ac detestabilis: And yet there are a
number of inscriptions from which one might conclude that
Tiberius was held in respect and esteem, e. g. one from Capena,

32 A. D., (CIL XI. 3872, quoted ad LIV. 1), in which he is entitled the *best and most just emperor, preserver of his father-land;* two from Rome which call him *best and most just emperor,* CIL VI. 93, 3675 (cf. 30856); two from Rome calling him the *best emperor,* CIL VI. 902, 904; one from Anticaria (quoted ad L. 3), entitling him *emperor and preserver,* CIL II. 2038; one from Chersonesus in Sarmatia, calling him the *greatest emperor,* IGR 1. 864, also coins struck in commemoration of his kindness and his foresight: Ti. Caesar divi Aug. f. August. imp. VIII, clementiae, s. c.: Cohen 1, p. 189. 4; Ti. Caesar Aug. pont. max., provident., per. Aug.: Cohen 1, p. 197. 84; cf. ib. 89, CIL XI. 4170 (quoted ad LXV. 2). At Aquila an aqueduct was built in his honor and that of his grandchildren: aquam August*am* | in honorem *Ti. Cae*|saris Augusti ne*po*tumque Pelt*vin.* | adduxer. pr. ae*tern.* Caesarum | Salvieni Paul*us et* | Florus | aed. qq. *ded.*: CIL IX. 4209. There are several dedications to the *genius* of Tiberius, CIL VI. 251 from Rome, 27 A. D., XI. 3076 from Falerii, XIII. 941 from Petrucorii (dedicated also to Jupiter, by the butchers). Besides these, very many inscriptions are dedicated to him, not for any particular act that is mentioned, but simply, it seems probable, out of general regard and honor: CIL II. 2037 (24 A. D.), 2062 (26 A. D.), 2181 (27 A. D.), all from Baetica; III. 7099 (34 A. D.) from Cyme, 12104 from Salamis (dedicated by the senate); V. 6417 from Ticinum, 8845 from Verona; IX. 3606 from Aveia, 4334 from the district of Amiternum (in fulfillment of a vow); X. 207 (15 A. D.) from Grumentum, 1414 (36 A. D.) from Herculaneum, 7226 (18 A. D.) from Lilybaeum, 8088 (32 A. D.) from Copia Thurii; XI. 2647 (15 A. D.) from Colonia Saturnia (set up by the seviri Augustales); XIII. 1590 from Ruessium, 1789 from Lugdunum, 4481 (20 A. D.) from Mediomatrici (dedicated by the tradesmen who lived there); XIV. 2592 (32 A. D.) from Tusculum, 2910 b from Praeneste, 3448 (33 A. D.) from Trevi, 3943 (34 A. D.) from Nomentum, 4176 (36 A. D.) from Lavinium; Eph. Ep. 8, p. 171. 708 from Naso in Sicily, p. 364. 22 from Emerita in Lusitania; ib. 9, p. 384. 609 from Lanuvium; Rev. Arch. 18 (1911), p. 495. 629 from Ostia (in fulfillment of a vow); IGR. 1. 1011 from Crete, 1160 (31 A. D.), 1164 (32–38 A. D.), 1171 (22 A. D.), 1172 (32 A. D.), 1173, all from Egypt; 3. 845 from Cilicia (wherein he is called *founder and savior*), 941 (14–15 A.D.), 942 both from

Cyprus; 4. 71, 72 both from Mytilene, 683 from Sebasta, 714 from Blaundus, 1144 from Lindus, 1288 from Monghla, 1391 from Smyrna (before he became emperor); Curtius u. Adler 371 (calling him *benefactor and patron*, but even before his adoption). Several inscriptions honor Tiberius in connection with one or more persons: CIL III. 7117 from Ephesus, honoring at the same time Diana of Ephesus, Augustus, and the city of Ephesus; V. 6416 on a triumphal arch at Ticinum, together with nine others of Augustus and his family; XI. 3786 from Veii, dedicated also to Germanicus, 3790 from Veii to Tiberius and to Claudius; XIII. 1036 on a triumphal arch at Mediolanum Santonum, to Germanicus, Tiberius, and Drusus, son of Tiberius. It is quite true that such dedications may have been made in a spirit of flattery and fawning, or from a sense of necessity or awe (cf. *Aug.* LVII. 1); but in the absence of any conclusive evidence for such an assumption, it is quite justifiable and fair to believe that they were made with an honest feeling of appreciation and affection.

LXV. 1.

Seianum: (Cf. XXVI. 2.) A bronze coin from Bilbilis bears the name of Sejanus as colleague of Tiberius in his fifth consulship (31 A. D.): Ti. Caesar divi Augusti f. Augustus; mun(icipium) Augusta Bilbilis Ti. Caesare V. L. Aelio Seiano cos.: Cohen 1, p. 198. 97. This seems an exceptional honor, for a coin of the same town, minted in Tiberius's third consulship, omits the name of his colleague, Germanicus: cf. ib. 96. Sejanus is named as consul also in a fragmentary inscription from Rome, referring to some time after his condemnation, CIL VI. 10213. His name appears, too, in inscriptions from Rome of two of his freedmen, CIL VI. 6030, 10769.

LXV. 2.

oppressa coniuratione Seiani: An inscription from Interamna, 32 A. D., is interesting in its reference to the crushing of Sejanus, and to the rôle assigned Tiberius in the matter, quite different from that described by Suetonius: Saluti perpetuae Augustae | libertatique publicae | populi Romani. | genio municipi anno post | Interamnam conditam | DCCIIII ad Cn. Domitium|Ahenobarbum !!!!!! | !!!!! cos.   providentiae Ti. Caesaris Augusti nati ad aeternitatem | Romani nominis, sublato hoste

perniciosissimo p(opuli) R(omani), | Faustus Titius Liberalis VI
vir Aug. iter. | p(ecunia) s(ua) f(aciendum) c(uravit): CIL XI.
4170.   The name erased is that of M. Furius Camillus Scriboni-
anus (cf. *Claud*. XIII), and the *hostis perniciosissimus* is Sejanus.
Another inscription, from Crete, CIL III. 12036, to the divinity
and foresight of Tiberius and of the senate (quoted ad XXVI. 1,
statuas etc.), was dedicated on the day of the death of Sejanus
(cf. Tac. *Ann*. 6. 25. 5).

LXVIII. 4.

sine adiumento…medicorum: (Cf. LXXII. 3.)   Cf.
Vesp. XX on the little attention paid by the Emperor to his
health.   That Tiberius, however, employed the services of a
masseur in assisting him to preserve his good health may be
inferred from the following inscription from Rome, although a
different interpretation is possible: Ti. Iulio Aug. lib. | Xantho
tractatori | Ti. Caesaris et | divi Claudi | et subpraef. classis |
Alexandriae | Atellia Prisca uxor | et Lamyrus l. heredes. | v. a.
LXXXX: CIL 32775 (33131).   Sen. *Ep*. 66.53 and Mart. 3.
82. 13 seem to represent the services of the *tractator* or his feminine
counterpart as employed merely for pleasure.

LXIX.

Circa deos…neglegentior: We have at least two inscriptions in which Tiberius himself, though not as emperor, pays
respects to the gods, to Jupiter Optimus Maximus in CIL VI.
385 (quoted ad IX. 3 consul iterum), to Hercules Invictus in
CIL II. 1660 (quoted ad XV. 2 adoptatur etc.).

LXX. 1.

Coruinum Messalam: He is mentioned in CIL VI. 1375
from Rome, and in 31618 there seems to be a fragment of his
name on an elogium of his father.

LXXII. 3.

Chariclen medicum: (Cf. LXVIII. 4.)   Of this physician
of Tiberius we seem to have no inscription, but another, an ocu-
list, we know from this memorial: Thyrius Ti. Caesaris | Aug.
ser. Celadianus | medicus ocularius | pius parentium suorum
| vixit annos XXX | hic situs est in perpet.: CIL VI. 8909 from
Rome on the Via Latina.

LXXIII. 1.

obiit...XVII. Kal. Ap. Cn. Acerronio Proculo C. Pontio Nigr<in>o conss.: This statement of Suetonius and that of Tacitus (*Ann.* 6. 50. 7), which make March 16 the date of Tiberius's death, are verified by the Acta Arvalium for 38 A. D., which set March 18 as the day on which Gaius was called imperator, as against Dio 58. 28, who puts it ten days later: a. d. XV. K. Apriles | *Tau*rus Statilius Corvinus promagister collegii fratrum Arvalium *nomine* | quod hoc die C. Caesar Augustus Germanicus a senatu impera*tor appellatus est,* | *in* Capitolio Iovi, Iunoni, Minervae hostias maiores III inmol*avit, ante templum* | *n*ovom divo Augusto unam: CIL VI. 2028 c. A fragment of the Fasti recently discovered at Ostia also supports Suetonius's statement: Cn. Acerronius C. Pontiu*s* | ...XVII. K. Apr. Ti. Caesar Misen*i* | excessit: Notizie degli Scavi, vol. XIV (1917), p. 182. The names of the consuls for the year appear also in an inscription from Lusitania, CIL II. 172. CIL X. 6774 from the island of Pontia is dedicated to Nigrinus, and his name appears again in a fragment from Rome, CIL VI. 9338. Proculus was honored with a statue under which appeared the following inscription: ὁ δῆμος | Γναῖον 'Ακερρώνιον | Πρόκλον ἀνθύπατον | τῆς εἰς ἑαυτὸν εὐνοίας | καὶ κηδεμονίας ἕνεκα | —Πραξιτέλης ἐποίη[σεν]: CIA 3. 1.611.

LXXV. 3.

corpus...Romam...deportatum est...: This statement, too, is supported by the above-mentioned, recently found inscription from Ostia: IIII. K. Apr. corpus | in urbe perlatum per mili*tes*; | III. Non. Apr. f(unere) p(ublico) e(latus) e(st). The inscription marking the spot where Tiberius's remains were deposited in Rome has survived: ossa | Ti. Caesaris divi Aug. f. | Augusti | pontificis maximi, | trib. pot. XXXIIX, imp. VIII, cos. V: CIL VI. 885.

LXXVI.

Tiberium: He was not permitted long to enjoy even the inferior position assigned him (cf. *Cal.* XXIII. 3), and but a brief inscription from Rome marks his tomb: Ti. Caesar | Drusi Caesaris f. | hic situs est: CIL VI. 892.